NO BULLSH*T PROJECT

A Project Manager's Guide to Successful Project Leadership

By

Kyle Nitchen

© **Copyright 2024 by Kyle Nitchen, All rights reserved.**

The content contained within this book may not be reproduced, duplicated, or transmitted without direct written permission from the author or the publisher.

Under no a will any blame or legal responsibility be held against the publisher or author for any damages, reparation, or monetary loss due to the information contained within this book. Either directly or indirectly.

Legal Notice:

This book is copyright-protected. This book is only for personal use. You cannot amend, distribute, sell, use, quote, or paraphrase any part of the content within this book without the consent of the author or publisher.

Disclaimer Notice:

Please note the information contained within this document is for educational and entertainment purposes only. All effort has been executed to present accurate, up-to-date, and reliable, complete information. No warranties of any kind are declared or implied. Readers acknowledge that the author is not engaging in the rendering of legal, financial, medical, or professional advice. The content within this book has been derived from various sources. Please consult a licensed professional before attempting any techniques outlined in this book.

By reading this document, the reader agrees that under no circumstances is the author responsible for any losses, direct or indirect, which are incurred as a result of the use of the information contained within this document, including, but not limited to, — errors, omissions, or inaccuracies.

Contents

INTRODUCTION 1
CHAPTER ONE 5
   The Seven Archetypes 5
CHAPTER TWO 13
   The Communicator 13
   9 Principles that Support Clear Communication 16
   Tool #1 The Minto Pyramid Principle 25
   Tool #2 Prioritize & Delegate 31
   Tool #3 The DISC Profile 37
   Tool #4 Write Like an Amazonian 48
   Chapter Takeaways 53
CHAPTER THREE 54
   The Enforcer 54
   Tool #1 Creating a Culture of Accountability 59
   Tool #2: Create a Compelling Scoreboard 65
   Tool #3 Begin Using Zero Tolerance 67
   Chapter Takeaways 69
CHAPTER FOUR 70
   The Builder 70
   Tool #1 The Eight Deadly Wastes 74
   Tool #2 The Last Planner System 75
   Tool #3 A Beginner's Guide to Understand MEP 80
   Chapter Takeaways 97
CHAPTER FIVE 98
   The Leader 98
   The 4 Stages Of Team Development 103
   Tool #1 Creating a Culture of Extreme Ownership 108
   Tool #2 Be the Captain Your Team Needs 109
   Tool #3 Emotional Intelligence 116
   Tool #4 6 Proven Ways to Increase Your Influence 125
   Chapter Takeaways 133

CHAPTER SIX 134
- The Attorney 134
- Characteristics of a Great Attorney 135
- Tool #1 Don't Skip Understanding the Project. 137
- Tool #2 The Risk & Opportunity Register 140
- How to Utilize a Risk & Opportunity Register 142
- Tool #3 The Biggest Risk Is You 144
- Chapter Takeaways 149

CHAPTER SEVEN 151
- The Accountant 151
- Tool #1 Accounting Practices for the Construction Industry 154
- Tool #2 Change Management 156
- Tool #3 Forecasting – The Art of Financial Foresight 163
- The Liquidity Indicator 169
- The Right Behaviors for Positive Cash Flow 171
- How to Accelerate Your Project's Profitability 173
- Conclusion 176
- Chapter Takeaways 176

CHAPTER EIGHT 178
- The Business Developer 178
- How to Build Relationships 181
- What is a Relationship? 181
- How to Quantify a Relationship 182
- Tool #1 The 4 Components to a Relationship 183
- Tool #2 Business Development in 11 Words 185
- Tool #3 Storytelling 190
- Tool #4 Be The Guide, Not The Hero 191
- Chapter Takeaways 192

CONCLUSION 194
BIBLIOGRAPHY 197

INTRODUCTION

Most project outcomes are, let's face it, bullsh*t. And I mean that in the most technical sense.

Bullsh*t can be described as a bunch of words and plans that ultimately mean nothing. And for the most part, projects can be described that way too. We all know it—schedules that tell us who does what by when but say nothing about the "how." Constant communication breakdowns. Lack of accountability and ownership. Large groups of people working together without trust or respect. Budgets that are constantly blown. Risks that no one is aware of or knows how to manage. And customers left unsatisfied with outcomes and benefits that never come to fruition.

Projects are the backbone of any economy, enabling power, travel, work, healing, entertainment, rapid communication, and security for the population. Despite their immense value, only three in 10 projects and one in 200 megaprojects are delivered on schedule, within budget, and meet their intended value. This pattern has to stop.

Consider the scenario in the following paragraph, and ask yourself, does this sound familiar?

Imagine staring at your email inbox, eyes burning from the strain of being up late again. Another fire to put out, another crisis pushing your project over budget. The chaos around you has become the new normal. You're stressed, exhausted, and overwhelmed.

Here's the truth.

No one told you that being a project manager meant drinking from a fire hose every day. The building process is filled with variations and unknowns. Owners expect projects to be completed at lightning speed and within budget. You have to juggle communication with teams and clients, budget for unforeseen problems, and constantly deal with poorly defined objectives, fragmented processes, and unrealistic client expectations. If you don't know what you're doing, you'll get stuck in a cycle of rush, push, and panic.

No wonder 41% of project managers are considering leaving the profession. Within the 2020s, a startling 25 million project managers will be needed due to mass retirements, while more professionals choose to leave their careers every day. The industry continues to grow, but project managers continue to walk away.

Things cannot keep going this way. This book was written specifically for project professionals. Know that every word you hear is meant to be heard as if we're speaking directly to you. Think about what you're hearing and try to apply it to your project management style. If you allow these lessons to influence your way of thinking, you will see immediate results in your effectiveness as a project manager.

Right now, you might feel overwhelmed, tired, and maybe even wondering if it will ever get any better. Trust me, I've been there.

But, what if project management could be clear, simple, efficient, successful, and actually fun? That's what No Bullsh*t Project is all about. It sweeps away all the complex and chaotic practices to leave you with pure, actionable project leadership skills.

I typically see four types of project managers.

1. **The Victim:** A victim doesn't understand what is going wrong and lacks the ability to fix it.

2. **The Witness:** A witness monitors problems and tracks them.
3. **The Manager:** A manager will see problems and react to fix them.
4. **The Leader:** A leader will anticipate problems in the future and do what it takes to prevent them.

In this book, you'll learn how to stop being a project victim, witness, or manager and start becoming a project leader. The one everyone seeks for their projects.

I'm going to show you a whole new set of behaviors, habits, skills, and strategies to help you plan with ease, control your risk, manage stakeholders, and lead your team. No Bullsh*t project can help you 30x your results by pure thought alone.

Imagine a career where you wake up every day feeling fulfilled, ready to take on any challenge. Instead of stressful mornings and restless nights, you approach your projects with confidence. What if every project was predictable, successful, on time, and within budget? You sit at your desk with a sense of calm, knowing you have the tools and systems to deal with problems, clients, and complexity. Gone are the days of being an overwhelmed administrative project manager.

Now, you're a strategic project leader.

With this knowledge and awareness, your job isn't the most stressful thing in your life. You feel fulfilled at work, seeing how your efforts benefit your community, career, and bank account.

Sound impossible?

It isn't. Trust me.

Over the years, I've gathered hundreds of unique project management techniques by leading over $450M+ in complex construction projects and collaborating with some of the sharpest minds in the industry.

In this book, you'll learn the exact framework that shows you how to navigate the industry with confidence. No more late and overbudget projects or irate clients. Now, you'll be in the top 1% of leaders who can tackle complex construction with distinction.

You don't have to get stuck in the usual bullsh*t of project management.

You can rise above.

It's time to learn and implement successful project leadership.

CHAPTER ONE

The Seven Archetypes

"Plans are nothing; planning is everything."

~ Dwight D. Eisenhower

Construction is complex, and many factors influence the outcome of a construction project. The job of a construction project manager is to take a set of written plans and specifications and a raw piece of land and then coordinate all of the materials, manpower, and equipment necessary to guarantee a set price, schedule, and quality of a project—without any accidents or errors, regardless of weather conditions, interest rate fluctuations, acts of God, or any other unforeseen conditions. *(Whew!)*

A top project manager must play many roles. You organize millions of dollars, millions of components, and lead hundreds of people. You lead meetings, negotiate contracts, control risks, update schedules, monitor budgets, solve problems, communicate with every stakeholder, develop people, and more. You set expectations and ensure they are met. With so much at stake, project managers must be well trained.

Anything and everything that needs to be done to build complex construction projects falls on your shoulders.

There are many ways to lead, but for a project manager who wants to excel, the 7 Archetypes serve as a solid foundation.

I've broken this book up into seven major archetypes that every project manager should master. Think of these archetypes as different roles that you play in the day-to-day process of leading a construction project. Each chapter is full of real-life scenarios, tools, and action plans to help you master these archetypes.

The seven archetypes is the ultimate framework for navigating the complexities of project management and developing into a successful project leader who consistently produces predictable outcomes. I've coached and helped hundreds of project leaders improve their outcomes using this framework. I have not yet found a better method than the 7 archetypes to become a well-rounded project manager—the type every organization seeks for their projects.

If you can learn to play these roles seamlessly, you'll be more prepared to tackle a construction project than 99% of project managers. You'll be able to lead people and predict outcomes.

Ready to get started?

Let's talk about the seven different archetypes.

What Is an Archetype?

An archetype is a typical example, pattern, or model that represents a specific role or behavior.

In project management, archetypes are the different roles you need to play to be effective. Each archetype provides a framework for specific actions and skills needed to succeed.

We'll explore each archetype and guide you on how to embody them effectively so you can successfully deliver your projects.

The Communicator

Success begins with clear communication. You cannot lead others if you cannot adequately share your thoughts and ideas with them.

It's not just about talking; it's about actively listening and tailoring your messages to your audience's needs.

Good communication prevents misunderstandings and gets everyone working off the same plan.

The Enforcer

The Enforcer is not a friend, a pal, or a coach. You cannot use your buddy status with the Enforcer. The Enforcer is the guy the team knows will not compromise on key policies or values.

They know that if they push, there will be push-back. Cross the line, and consequences follow, especially for things like safety, cleanliness, timeliness, schedule, and accountability.

A PM who can't or won't take on the Enforcer role is going to deal with a lot of complications while trying to be only the good guy.

The Builder

The central figure that ensures quality construction work takes place.

The Builder has in-depth knowledge of how to use various construction materials, methods, and building systems.

They can see what's not on the plans, create solutions, fix problems across different trades, and organize work efficiently to reduce waste and maximize value.

The Leader

The most influential and visible way everyone on the project learns is by watching The Leader.

The Leader is a selfless, dedicated individual who prioritizes the team and its goals over personal interests.

As natural motivators, they build an environment that produces future leaders and inspires passion and dedication.

The Attorney

In construction, contracts bind us all, and understanding the legal side is crucial.

The Attorney navigates contracts, legal obligations, and risk management.

Their expertise helps the team understand these complexities and manage risks to keep the project compliant.

The Accountant

Handling millions in finances means the margin for error is minimal.

The Accountant is skilled in preparing and maintaining key financial information.

With expertise in forecasting and budgeting, they manage risk, make great decisions, and keep their profit.

The Business Developer

Future projects are just as important as the current one.

The Business Developer, both authentic and likable, focuses on building lasting relationships and understanding clients' needs, leading to ongoing success.

Your Hero's Journey

Mastering these roles won't equip you to solely building great establishments. You'll build the career, life, team, and community that you want.

The closer work feels like play, the more we feel we are thriving.

To get into flow in all aspects of work, you need a good scorecard. Change is a sustained reinforcement of new behaviors and thinking patterns.

The 7 archetypes provide a clear framework to gauge and refine your management approach.

This book will give you the tools to evaluate your proficiency in these crucial behavior patterns (and your teams') so you can decide where you want to make changes and improve.

Round Wheels Roll Best

Before we jump into the specifics for each archetype, use the wheel below to assess your strengths and weaknesses. Doing so will help you evaluate yourself, build awareness, and improve one area at a time.

NO BULLSH*T PROJECT

THE 7 ARCHETYPES

THE 7 ARCHETYPES PROVIDE A CLEAR FRAMEWORK TO
GAUGE AND REFINE YOUR MANAGEMENT APPROACH.

THINK ABOUT THE 7 CATEGORIES BELOW,
AND RATE THEM FROM 1 - 10.

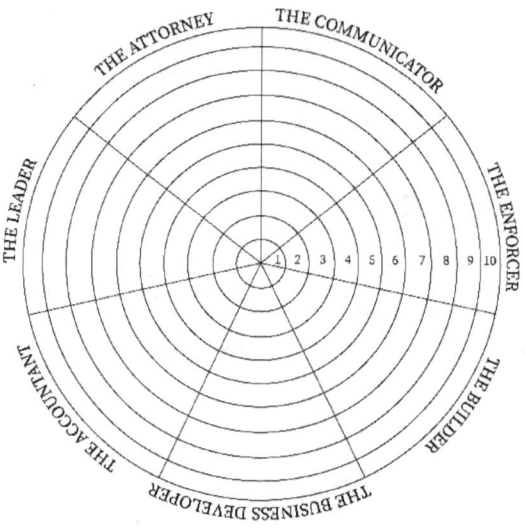

KYLENITCHEN.COM

Here's a step-by-step guide to using the wheel.

1. **Assessment Wheel:** Visualize the center of a wheel as 0 and the outer edges as 10.
2. **Rate Yourself:** Assign a number to each archetype based on your satisfaction. Shade the section to represent the score.
3. **Analyze Your Wheel:** Most wheels aren't perfectly round, meaning some areas need more attention.
4. **Focus:** Choose up to two areas to work on. It is hard to make improvements in many places at once.
5. **Define Success:** Ask, "What does a score of 9 or 10 represent in each section?" By doing this, you visualize your ultimate goal.

6. **Set Time-bound Goals:** Allocate a realistic timeframe to achieve these objectives.
7. **Make it a Game:** Aim for a score of 10 in every section. Stay true to your goals and avoid being swayed by others.
8. **Team Effort:** If you lead a team, engage them in this exercise. Revisit and evaluate together 1-2 times per year to track progress.

Remember, round wheels roll best!

Through becoming a more well-rounded and influential project manager, we can build a better world.

Let's begin.

Want to read more about becoming an influential project leader? Scan the QR code below to sign up for my free weekly newsletter! Every Tuesday, get one strategic idea, framework, tip, or tool delivered straight to your inbox to help you lead successful projects with confidence.

NO BULLSH*T PROJECT

CHAPTER TWO

The Communicator

The single biggest problem in communication is the illusion that it has taken place.

~George Bernard Shaw

I remember a project manager who couldn't get the plan out of his head. He was constantly stressed and running around, trying to figure out what was going on. I remember thinking what he needed most was a piece of paper, a pen, and a good coordination meeting with his team. He constantly told me he just didn't know how to get the plan out of his head.

After a few days of helping him, we were able to create a detailed project schedule that visually showed all the parts and pieces of the plan. The team loved it and bought into it right away. Even then, he admitted that he still felt uncomfortable, despite the project becoming more stable. His assistant project manager took charge of the plan, regularly updating and communicating it with the team. Eventually, the project manager was removed from the project and later told me he didn't think he belonged in project management at all.

Either get the plan out of your head and onto paper, with your team, or suffer in chaos. As a project manager, it's your job to ensure *everyone* is on the same page working off the same plan. And the best way to do that is by becoming an excellent communicator.

Why Does a Project Manager Need to Be a Great Communicator?

In project management, you are constantly leading teams of people to a desired outcome. You're communicating with clients, subcontractors, and employees. You are the conduit of which all communication flows through. Not communicating the plan in a clear, visual way is a waste of time and money for everyone involved. It creates chaos and wastes an incalculable amount of time.

Setting clear expectations, decision making, resolving conflicts, managing stakeholders, managing team performance, reducing misunderstandings and errors, adapting to change, and promoting accountability all have one thing in common—communication.Effective communication is a crucial element of successful project management.

In this chapter, we'll discuss the characteristics of a great communicator, and three tools you can use to build your communication skills: the Minto Pyramid Principle, CPQQRT, and the DISC Profile.

Archetype #1 – The Communicator

The first archetype we're going to cover in this book is *The Communicator*.

The communicator is someone who delivers their message clearly and is receptive and responsive to others' input.

The communicator has the superpower of deep listening and can hear and address the true message of what's being said, even when the speaker is stifled in their expression.

You can improve your communication skills with practice much more effectively than you can improve your intelligence with practice. If you're not that smart but can communicate ideas clearly, you have a great advantage over everybody who can't communicate clearly.

Great communicators are highly respected and trusted. They're known for becoming the go-to source for other people on their projects and within their organization.

Getting to this point and becoming an excellent project manager really boils down to mastering the art of "Clear Communication."

What is Clear Communication?

Clear Communication is when the idea in my mind and the idea in your mind is the exact same after I communicate it to you.

To put it simply, when you use Clear Communication, there is nothing lost in translation.

The best communicators also change the mode of communication to fit the listener's needs (communicating one-on-one, via email, in a meeting, or through some other method as needed), and successfully navigate the obstacles of working in virtual teams. These people have developed the skill of not just relaying their message but choosing the best method for it to be transmitted.

A high score in the Clear Communication category indicates the ability to get to the point clearly and concisely over many different mediums. You are skilled at transmitting ideas and put in effort to understand others. This ability is a powerful asset for developing people skills and executing projects. Clear Communicators are likely accomplished collaborators, more productive with their time, experience lower turnover, and skilled at achieving buy-in. Here are nine principles that you can use in your day-to-day work to become a Clear Communicator

9 Principles that Support Clear Communication

Let's talk about the nuts and bolts of how you communicate to ensure that your message and your meaning are clear.

1. Identify Your Key Message

The first thing you can do is identify your key message before every interaction. Your key message is the most important point, idea, action, or feeling you want people to take away from this interaction with you. This is going to help guide the interaction and the way you present your ideas.

In professional settings, you may think about what you want the other person to learn, to know, or to understand from listening to you.

In personal situations, you may simply want to connect with the other person or learn something about a new friend or acquaintance.

You want to focus on this key message, or the overall idea or impression that you want the other person to leave with.

It's about making sure that the other person leaves the conversation, meeting, or presentation with something that stood out to them, something memorable.

Coming back to this key message again and again helps you stay focused. It helps you ensure that you're communicating your meaning clearly because you have a specific goal in mind.

2. Knowledge & Preparation

This may be obvious to some, but prepare and rehearse ahead of time. Know what you are going to say and how you are going to say it before you begin any type of communication.

Being prepared means more than just practicing a presentation. Preparation involves thinking about the entirety of the communication, from start to finish. Research the information you may need to support your message. Consider how you will respond to questions and criticisms. Try to anticipate the unexpected. My favorite way to do this is by writing my message out beforehand. For complex topics, I like to create visuals. It helps me understand the content. If I can understand it, I can help others understand it, too.

3. Active Listening

Active listening is a superpower for both communication and leadership.

When you look at all the traits of people in the highest leadership and management positions, active listening is a common shared skill. People feel inspired and motivated when they have leaders who listen to them.

Listening builds trust, creates transparency, and fosters loyalty. It also gives leaders insight to the stress and tension points of those they lead. Active listening encourages stronger communication between leaders and team members and drives engagement.

Active listening means giving your full attention to a person who is speaking. An active listener focuses on the person they're communicating with, expresses interest, and meaningfully engages in the conversation. You must be listening both verbally and non-verbally in your communication.

Here are seven techniques you can immediately implement to improve your active listening skills.

1. **Focus on the intent and purpose of the conversation.** This will help you truly understand and empathize with them. **Don't** daydream or interrupt. Just **listen to** the content. That way, the listener and speaker build an authentic connection.
2. **Pay attention to body language.** Body language refers to the conscious and unconscious gestures that express or convey information. Such behavior can include facial expressions, posture, hand gestures, eye contact or movement, and touch.
3. **Give encouraging verbal cues.** Verbal cues are prompts that a speaker may use to elicit a response or reaction from the listener. This includes small replies such as "yes, I see" or "mmhmm" or "I understand." These are often used alongside gestures and expressions, such as smiling or nodding.
4. **Clarify and paraphrase information.** Sometimes, it is not enough to nod and maintain eye contact in a conversation. You might have doubts about whether your mind grasped the full picture. Clarifying and paraphrasing the information back to the speaker can help both of you fill in any gaps in understanding.
5. **Ask questions.** Just like paraphrasing to clarify what a speaker has said, asking questions can eliminate confusion. As an active listener, you can also demonstrate interest by asking questions.
6. **Refrain from judgement.** When practicing active listening, it is important to remain open, neutral, and nonjudgmental. What's so wonderful about taking the steps to become a

better listener is that you can engage with new ideas, perspectives, and opportunities that you may never have accessed previously.
7. **Summarize, share, and reflect.** Toward the end of your interaction, make sure you end on a high note. Share a quick summary or a few notes about what the speaker said.

4. Understand First, Then Seek to Be Understood

The fifth habit of Stephen Covey's *The 7 Habits of Highly Effective People* is: *"Seek first to understand, then to be understood."*

When truly effective, interdependent people communicate, they first try to understand the other person's perspective before expressing their own.

It's easy to be quick to jump in with your position, saying what you need to say. It takes skill and intention to pause, collect information, and craft an appropriate response for better outcomes.

Here's a quick tip: know what kinds of questions will get you the answers you need. Oftentimes, it's easy for us to quickly ask "yes/no" questions, when what we're really searching for is a greater context.

As part of active listening, by seeking first to understand, you'll be in a better position to find Win-Win solutions to interpersonal problems, the trust in your relationships will increase significantly, and your circle of influence will expand.

5. Avoid Confusion, Be Clear and Concise

Get rid of the sentence-fillers. All those "ums" and "uhs" subconsciously come from a good place—linguists suggest that we use them to avoid uncomfortable silences while we search for the right words. However, these fillers can get in the way. They make us appear less confident and can work against us when we're trying to persuade others.

If you have a presentation, practice through the words you'll use to avoid the need for fillers. If you find yourself in a casual conversation and can't find the right words, try to catch yourself before the "um" slips out, and just pause instead. This can create more cohesion between your thoughts and keep your conversational partner from tuning out.

Write clear, straight-forward messages using plain language to avoid confusion or misunderstandings. Avoid wordiness by eliminating most adjectives and adverbs (very, really, extremely).

Keep your message brief to get to the point quickly. This means you must be selective with your information and pay special attention to how your phrasing can be worded in the most efficient way possible.

6. Use Visual Communication

This is a big one. We've all heard the cliché, "a picture tells a thousand words," but there is real value in using images to communicate complex content. Images help us learn, grab attention, explain tough concepts, and inspire.

Getting your message across in a clear, concise way can be difficult with words alone. Humans are naturally visual creatures. Visual communication is the practice of using visual elements to communicate information or ideas. By incorporating visuals, you can save a lot of back and forth due to confusion.

Visual communication plays an important role in establishing and maintaining a reliable workflow. When communication breaks down on a job site, teams will experience loss of productivity, hindered completion times, and costly errors. Visual communication tools will significantly help to bridge communication gaps and facilitate better trade-to-trade collaboration and accountability.

Here are four important reasons why visual communication works:

1. Visual communication saves time by relaying messages faster.
2. Visual communication ensures that a clear, unified message is delivered.
3. Visual communication helps to provide a shared, consistent experience.
4. Visual communication results in better retention of the information.

7. Use Proven Formatting Techniques

As project managers, we often have to communicate in writing. PMs who know how to write effectively have a major advantage.

Formatting is the easiest way you can 10x the impact of your written word.

In the writing world, almost all of the focus gets placed on the words themselves. "What are you saying? What's the idea? How beautiful is the language? Are the commas in the right places? Does the sentence flow? Should you use this adjective or that adjective?"

And yes, while all of these things matter (quite a bit), writers often forget that the way their words LOOK on the page drastically changes the way readers read and consume their work. In fact, the way your words LOOK on the page is usually what determines whether or not readers will take the time to read what you've written at all.

Formatting matters. Here are four points on how to better format your written communication to be better understood.

- Start every section with a single-sentence opener. Some examples are:

- Open with 1 strong, declarative sentence.
- Open with 1 thought-provoking question.
- Open with 1 vulnerable statement.
- Open with 1 unique insight.

- Always look for opportunities to turn long paragraphs into bulleted lists.

- Use sub-headings. Subheadings are bolded sentences throughout a piece that help the reader know "where" they are in your line of thinking.

- Use the 1 / 3 / 1 writing rhythm to keep readers engaged all the way down the page. 1 sentence, 3 sentences, 1 sentence. The key to injecting rhythm and skimmability into your writing is to alternate length of sentences and sections—opening and closing each section with a single sentence.

The key to formatting is to think about reducing friction for the reader. You should always be asking yourself, "How can I make this easier and more enjoyable for my readers?"

The recipient is the main character here. The reader is who matters most. So, to be an effective writer, you must be in service to them.

8. Balance The Science & Art of Communication

Being able to effectively and consistently communicate with different kinds of people requires a blend of both the scientific and artistic components of communication.

THE SCIENCE OF COMMUNICATION

It all starts with a strong grasp of how to structure your thoughts effectively in the language and dialect you're working with. If, while you're speaking, friends or coworkers often ask you to back up and repeat something you said, aren't sure how you got from Point A to

Point B, or give you a blank look like they're zoning out, it may help to revisit the basics.

1. ***Sentence Structure.*** For most of us, it's been a fair number of years since we've had to wonder about comma placement, ensuring our sentences don't run on, and the right spelling of there/their/they're. If you're having trouble communicating in person, try speaking in many short sentences instead of one long sentence. Check in with your conversational partner often for comprehension. Asking "Does this make sense?" or "Do you know what I need from you?" will help ensure you're both on the same page with regards to next steps. If your emails don't seem to be getting your point across, try enhancing your writing skills by reading. Work on emulating the sentence structures you see in print.

2. ***Idea Structure.*** Knowing how to structure your sentences into a larger idea is essential. Even if you're delivering all the right information someone needs to know, if it's delivered in the wrong order, you risk the message not getting across. For example, if you put the main takeaway somewhere in the middle of a paragraph, what happens if your audience only had time to skim the email? They might come away from the email feeling like they understand, but not knowing what you need from them. Keep your words as succinct as possible to not detract from the point. From there, determine if it's appropriate to provide detail, backtrack, and answer questions.

9. Choosing the Right Communication Method

Communication takes many forms, including verbal, non-verbal, written, and visual. All these forms of communication are essential, and it's important to understand how to use them effectively.

Think about a person on your project team who does not seem to understand the team's goal even after multiple communications. Try a different communication channel. Different people process information in different ways.

Let's say you have sent her an email five times and she keeps asking you questions that are clearly answered in the email. Some people are visual; they might want to see a chart, so try sending that person a chart. Other people are verbal and will do much better from a conversation. If you're in an environment where you can do so, walk down the hallway and sit in front of her. If you're in a virtual environment, call her on the phone. It is the communicator's responsibility to find the correct medium for the message, so it is best understood by the recipient.

The success of the entire project leans on the fact that everyone involved knows what they are to do, how it is to be accomplished, and when it needs to be completed. They also need to know where to go and how to convey when an issue arises.

It's a juggling act of verbal, non-verbal, written, and visual communication, plus listening skills to engage and move things along. A great project manager will be in tune with all of this detail and know how to manage as things change.

By mastering the foundations of language with the art of tailoring your message to the audience, you'll communicate more clearly and effectively than ever.

Now, let's take a look at the different tools for The Communicator.

Tool #1 The Minto Pyramid Principle

Last year, I adopted a new structure to my communication, and the results were shocking.

My communication instantly became more clear and efficient.

This transformation is thanks to the Minto Pyramid Principle, a method developed by Barbara Minto, a former McKinsey & Company consultant. Today, it's a key tool for effectively conveying complex information in consulting, business, and government organizations.

The Minto Pyramid Principle organizes communication hierarchically. At its core, it begins with your **central message**, then branches out into **supporting ideas**, and finally, ends with the **detailed data**.

Imagine a pyramid: the wide base represents all the nitty-gritty details, and as you go up, the information gets consolidated into more general points, with the most important, overarching idea at the top.

In the context of construction project management, where complex concepts are the norm, the Minto Pyramid Principle can be an essential daily tool. When crafting a message or document, lead with your conclusion, support it with key points, and then back up those points with detailed evidence.

This method presents information in a top-down fashion, ensuring your main points are front and center. Begin with your conclusion to capture attention, then unpack the reasoning and data to reinforce your message.

By applying this principle to your business communications, including everything from emails to project reports, you can improve your clarity and effectiveness. Clear communication is often the hallmark of great leadership.

As demonstrated, I've led with the main idea: **Clarity is king.**

That's the beauty of the Minto Pyramid Principle—getting straight to the point. Ready for a deeper dive? Let's explore how to master this tool for everyday use.

What is the Pyramid Principle?

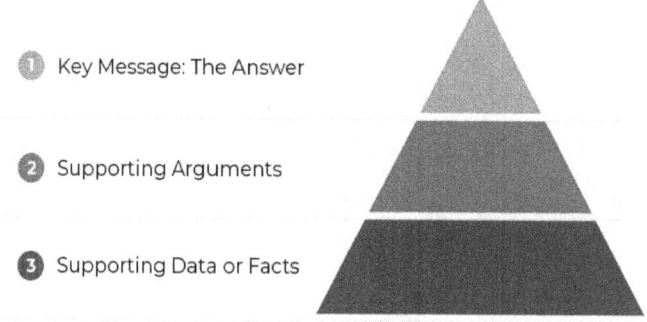

While at McKinsey, Minto noticed that people, in general, were terrible at constructing compelling arguments. She also noticed that people have busy minds and their attention spans are limited.

Their arguments lacked structure and focused too much on presenting data and facts upfront. As a result, by the time they reached their final recommendation, the audience had already lost interest or become distracted by the details.

Minto realized that unlike how you usually tell a good story, where you build suspense by delaying the resolution of a key issue until the very end, in a business presentation context you should do the exact opposite: Lead with the answer.

Your colleagues or stakeholders don't need to be entertained; they're busy and want to get things done. So, the simple solution is to lead with the answer.

This is what is known as the Pyramid Principle:

1. Start with the recommendation/answer/solution upfront
2. Back up that recommendation with a handful of supporting arguments
3. Build trust in your arguments using supporting data

If you do, this the structure of your argument ends up looking like a pyramid:

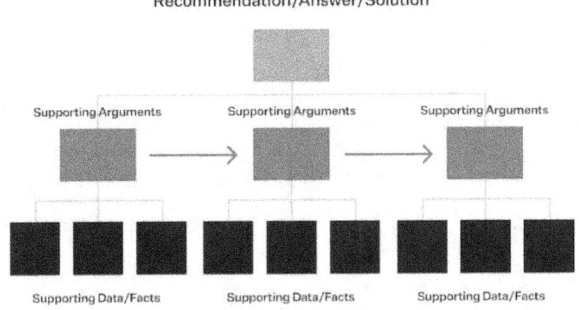

It's the exact opposite of what most of us are naturally drawn to—the upside-down-pyramid:

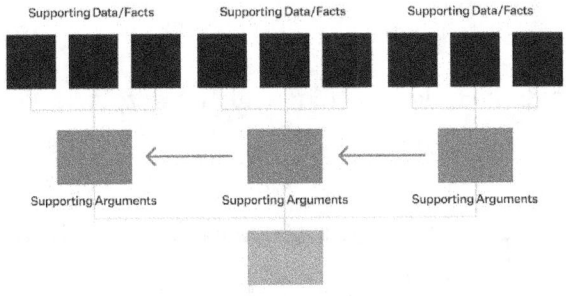

Most people, consciously or unconsciously, tend to use the upside-down pyramid when presenting complex information. This is how we think and process information. We build up to a conclusion by first reciting all of the facts, recounting all of the analyses that have been done, or reviewing all of the supporting ideas. Then, we get to the punch line.

However, effective communication and thinking are not done in the same way. As Minto put it, *"You think from the bottom up, but you present from the top down."*

Applying the Pyramid Principle will enable you to present your thinking so clearly that the ideas move off the page and into the reader's mind with minimum effort and maximum effect.

It's time to bring your ideas to life!

Step 1: Lead with the Answer

In construction project management, time is of the essence, much like in consulting firms such as McKinsey, where the mantra is to "lead with the answer."

If a project stakeholder asks, "What is your solution to this problem?", a construction manager should promptly reply with, "We need to focus on X." State your conclusion first, then explain your reasoning if required.

Here's why this method works well:

1. **Saves Time:** Stakeholders often juggle numerous tasks and value concise communication. They want to grasp the essentials rapidly. If you present your main point right away, you can capture their interest immediately, and they may agree without further details.
2. **Focuses on Core Objectives:** Executives and senior project leaders look for solutions that align with the project's

primary goals. By leading with your main suggestion, you cater to their preference for focusing on key strategies, rather than getting bogged down in details.
3. **Increase Influence:** A clear, direct recommendation reflects confidence. When you assert your proposed action decisively, you come across as more convincing and authoritative.

Step 2: Supporting Arguments

After presenting your answer, be prepared with supporting arguments. These are the facts and rationale that reinforce your main point.

Several types of supporting arguments can be used to strengthen a case. These include:

- **Data and Facts:** Leverage concrete numbers such as project timelines, cost estimates, or material quantities to substantiate your recommendations.
- **Supporting Evidence:** Reference relevant studies, such as structural assessments or workflow analyses, which can provide empirical backing to your main points.
- **Logical Reasons:** Use clear, straightforward reasoning that connects directly to project goals—like how a particular building method aligns with your efficiency objectives.
- **Financials and Performance Metrics:** Show how your proposal stands up financially by discussing budget implications, ROI, or performance metrics, such as expected improvement in construction timelines or reduction in waste.

Step 3: Supporting Data and Facts

Solid evidence is essential to back up your main point and make your argument convincing. Facts, stats, and real-world examples like case studies give weight to your ideas and show they work in practice.

Examples of supporting data and facts include:

- **Market Analysis:** Use specific construction market trends or needs analysis to justify a new building project or the adoption of a new construction method.
- **Project Case Studies:** Cite examples of similar construction projects that succeeded due to a similar approach or solution, emphasizing the outcomes relevant to your current project.
- **Financial Projections:** Provide cost-benefit analyses, budget forecasts, or financial impacts to showcase the economic advantage or cost savings of your recommended actions.

Remember...

Clear communication is the key to success, especially in project management.

The Pyramid Principle keeps things simple yet impactful: start with your main idea, then lay out the supporting points and evidence like a well-structured blueprint. It's straightforward, no-frills, and gets results.

As project managers, you're the bridge between vision and reality. Adopting this principle means your team gets the clarity they need, decisions are made faster, and projects stay on track.

Give it a try, and you'll see how it streamlines your communication and brings your ideas to life!

Let's take a look at another helpful tool for communicating.

Tool #2 Prioritize & Delegate

To delegate, you must remember to select the person, discuss the task, clearly define expectations, and give them time to execute the task.

Then, you check in on them periodically and help them accomplish the task, if necessary. Appropriately and professionally holding them accountable to expectations and the deadline is crucial.

Not delegating or not being able to delegate is a project leadership sin because:

1. The leader must be steering the ship or the fleet and be focused on being a good captain. This cannot be done if the would-be leader is down below doing lower-level chores that he or she was unable to delegate; and
2. A senior level leader must mentor others. You cannot mentor others if they are never given the chance to perform tasks and learn.

To help you determine what to delegate versus what to keep as your task, I often refer to the Eisenhower Matrix.

Quadrant 1: Do

When you see a task on your to-do list that must be done now, has clear consequences, and affects your long-term goals, place it in this quadrant.

Quadrant 2: Schedule

When you see a task on your to-do list that affects your long-term goals but doesn't have clear consequences, you can schedule these tasks for later. You'll tackle these tasks right after you tackle the tasks in quadrant one. These are the tasks that are the toughest to complete and will give the most resistance because there are no clear consequences. The only thing that will suffer if you don't do them is your future.

Quadrant 3: Delegate

When you see a task on your to-do list that must be done now but doesn't require your specific skill set or expertise, you can delegate to other members of your team. These tasks must be completed now, but they don't affect your long-term goals.

Quadrant 4: Delete

When you have gone through your to-do list and placed tasks in the above three quadrants, you'll see a set of tasks that are left over. These are tasks that weren't urgent or important. These types of tasks are simply getting in your way of accomplishing your goals. These go in the fourth quadrants, which are to be deleted.

Remarkable things will begin to happen on your projects and in your life when you start controlling what quadrant you are operating in.

You do only those things that are important to the project. And you delegate everything else!

The Ultimate Delegation Tool

CPQQRT might not roll off the tip of your tongue, but it is a great mnemonic for understanding and clarifying the required elements of a task, both for the person assigning the task and the person it is assigned to.

The task is in the mind of the manager and the framework is a tool to support the communication of this to someone else. If the Manager cannot write down or articulate what they want from the task—then how can anyone else be expected to deliver on it?

When your direct reports are clear about what they are being asked to do and why, they are much more likely to deliver what you want, when you want it, and with minimal requirements for your time along the way.

Clear articulation of the task, activity, or plan using this tool allows for a greater level of understanding and clarity between the task giver and task receiver.

What is CPQQRT?

CPQQRT is six prompts for the things that you should address when briefing a team member on a new task:

- **C**ontext
- **P**urpose
- **Q**uality
- **Q**uantity
- **R**esources
- **T**ime

It was developed by Elliot Jaques, a Canadian organizational psychologist, and first referenced in 1994 in the book *Executive leadership: A Practical Guide to Managing Complexity*.

CPQQRT is a core tool that supports project and team member success.

It ensures our communication is clear, comprehensive, and complete.

Let's look at each element of the CPQQRT tool in detail.

Setting Context

Context aims at setting the scene and providing clarity about what brought about the task, linkages to other tasks, and anything that could in any substantive way influence what we are trying to achieve.

Questions to ask:

- Why is this important?
- Who is concerned?
- What is the history?

Defining Purpose

This is the reason for the work—not the work itself.

It clarifies why we are doing this and what do we hope to achieve by doing so.

Questions to ask:

- What is the overarching "why"?
- What do you want this project or task to do or not do?
- How will you know the goal will be achieved?

Describing Quality

Quality can be described in more general terms. For example, within industry, safety, or environmental standards.

Quality can also have a relationship angle as in: achieve XYZ and establish a working relationship with stakeholder ABC.

Questions to ask:

- In what format?
- What will the output be like?
- What level of detail is required?

Describing Quantity

This can be tricky for more complex tasks, but it refers to the output in numbers and answers the question: how many?

Questions to ask:

- How long?
- How many?

Identifying Resources

These are the resources that will be available to deliver the task to the desired quantity/quality and include:

- Money (budget)

- Equipment (e.g., software, whiteboards, AV)
- Meeting rooms
- People and their availability (e.g., Board, Exec, Staff)
- External support (if applicable)
- Project sponsor/manager and their availability
- Central support (e.g., PMO, IT, Admin)

Establishing Time

The final element is about establishing detailed timelines for the project—when activities need to be completed, by what date, and what time frames are available for each stage of the project.

Remember, ASAP is not a date and is never clear enough.

Questions to ask:

- What is the last responsible moment?
- What are the fixed deadlines?
- What is the lead time required for each step?
- How frequently should follow ups be?

By using the CPQQRT tool, you can clearly communicate the context, purpose, quality standards, quantity, required resources, and time frame for delegating a task or resolving a complex issue.

The Readback

After you have delivered the CPQQRT, one of the best tools to implement is a readback. A readback is when the receiver repeats the message they just heard to ensure it was understood accurately.

Whether you're giving information or receiving information, this tool allows you to catch alignment errors before they happen and prevent costly resources from being put toward the wrong priorities.

A readback isn't a test of their listening skills. It's a test of your communication skills. Even in simple two-way communication, the sender must verify with the receiver that not only was the content of their message received, but the intent of the message was understood fully.

Try this tool out and see the difference they can make in how things get done.

Let's take a look at the third tool for effective communication.

Tool #3 The DISC Profile

Building healthy and successful relationships starts with self-awareness. Before joining a team, it is important you understand your strengths, weaknesses, communication style, and stress responses, then guide your team on effectively interacting with you.

The DISC profile is a behavioral assessment tool that categorizes individuals into four primary personality types:

(1) Dominance (D),
(2) Influence (I),
(3) Steadiness (S)
(4) Conscientiousness (C).

Once you understand these traits and the reasoning behind them, you'll be able to adapt to the styles of those around you, better communicate, improve team dynamics, and grow as a leader.

Self-Awareness: The Root of Healthy Relationships

We don't see things as they are. We see things as we are.

~Anais Nin

It is very important that you know who you are before you become a member of a team.

Now, that might sound a little silly because you think you already know yourself, but there are specific strengths, weaknesses, and tendencies you may take for granted that will come to bear when connecting with your team.

It is important that you know your strengths and weaknesses, your style of communication, how you behave under stress, and share with the team how best to interact with you effectively.

There are many different ways to self-discover and communicate who you are. The **DISC Model** is one of the best tools to quickly understand yourself and others.

What is DISC?

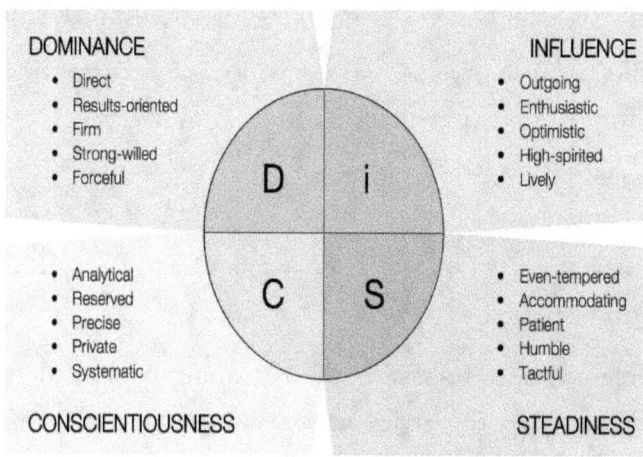

The DISC Personality Test is based on a theory introduced by Dr. William Marston in the 1920s. He wrote a book called *Emotions of Normal People* where he first mentioned the concept.

Marston believed that people generally exhibit a combination of four main behavior styles:

1. **D (Dominance):** People who are confident and like taking charge.
2. **I (Influence):** People who are social and enjoy being around others.
3. **S (Steadiness):** People who are calm, patient, and like things to stay the same.
4. **C (Conscientiousness):** People who pay attention to details and like things done correctly.

While Marston had the idea, he didn't create the test itself. In the 1970's, an industrial psychologist named Walter Clarke developed an assessment based on Marston's theory. Over time, others refined and adapted the test to what we see today.

The DISC test groups behavior into understandable categories. It doesn't say one style is better than another; instead, it highlights strengths and challenges of each type. Over the years, many professionals have used it and found it to be a useful tool to understand and predict behavior, especially in workplace settings.

The most reliable way to understand your own style is to take a DISC profile test. There are many DISC profile vendors online where you can take the DISC personality test either for free or at a relatively low cost. Here are some options:

- <u>123Test:</u> They offer a free DISC personality test that provides a brief overview of your profile.
- <u>DISC Personality Testing:</u> They offer a free test version and more detailed results for a small fee.
- <u>Tony Robbins' Website:</u> The renowned life coach offers a free DISC assessment on his website.

Revealing Your Hidden Genius Through DISC

I don't like that man. I'm going to have to get to know him better.

~Abraham Lincoln

In his book *The True Competitive Advantage*, Dan Silvert uses birds as metaphors to represent the DISC behavioral model.

Dan took the DISC model to another level by representing these characteristics as Eagles (D), Parrots (I), Doves (S), and Owls (C).

- Owls: Wisdom, analytical, smart
- Parrots: Colorful, talkative, fun
- Doves: Peace, harmony, kindness
- Eagles: Strong, dominant, power

Why use birds?

Because these colorful metaphors quickly reveal themselves as illuminating, memorable representations of the four styles in a fun and non-threatening way.

Each bird has a set of core traits. Once you understand these traits and the reasoning behind them, you'll be able to adapt to the styles of those around you, better communicate, improve team dynamics, and grow as a leader.

- An Eagle's primary focus is achieving results: they are decisive, direct, and action oriented. (Dominant)
- A Parrot's primary focus is social interaction: they are optimistic, fun seeking, and spontaneous. (Influential)
- A Dove's primary focus is building harmony: they are patient, sincere, and attentive. (Steady)
- An Owl's primary focus is achieving accuracy: they are detail oriented, systematic, and analytical. (Conscientious)

Understanding why people say and do the things they do depersonalizes difficult situations, handing you multiple keys to enter into a much more positive dynamic that reduces your stress.

To become better communicators and leaders, we're going to walk through each of Dan's bird (personality) types and see the world from each perspective.

Once we understand these different styles, we can stop creating delusions that give us permission to dislike people. Instead, we move beyond biases and value different viewpoints, creating a stronger team dynamic.

Eagles (D)

Eagles, represented by the "D" in the DISC model, are driven by their results-oriented nature. They're direct and decisive, always focused on achieving their objectives quickly and efficiently.

When communicating with an Eagle, it's beneficial to use words like "win," "powerful," "challenge," and "momentum." They're attracted to the idea of overcoming obstacles and value productivity and achievement.

However, vague terms such as "maybe" or "try" should be avoided, as Eagles thrive on clarity and decisive action.

Tips for Influencing an Eagle:
- Be brief.
- Be authentic.
- Avoid ambiguity.
- Focus on big picture objectives.
- Use action-oriented language and declarative sentences.
- Open with a problem that his or her participation can help solve.

- Keep your energy high, whether that means speaking or walking quickly.
- Sit or stand straight, make eye contact, and speak with confidence.

Leadership Priorities:
- Action Oriented: Focuses on progress through taking action.
- Clear Communication: Prioritizes brevity and clarity.
- Confidence: Utilizes self-assurance and grand visions to inspire others.
- Risk Taking: Will stretch what is possible to achieve a competitive advantage.

Leadership Weaknesses:
- Flexibility: Slow to listen or adopt other perspectives.
- Quality: Avoids drilling down into the details.
- Pacing: Chooses decisive action over planning.
- Focus: Prioritizes tasks over people.

Parrots (I)

Parrots, represented by the "I" in the DISC model, are vibrant personalities driven by their people-oriented and spontaneous nature. They are the life of the party, exuding optimism and a zest for fun in every interaction.

When engaging with a Parrot, using words like "fun," "exciting," "unique," and "innovative" will grab their attention. They thrive on new opportunities and adore anything that's fresh and different.

However, it's wise to avoid diving into intricate details or system-oriented discussions with them; they're less interested in the fine print and more in the broad strokes of an idea.

Tips for Influencing a Parrot:

- Talk a bit faster to pick up the energy.
- Be more informal in demeanor and dress.
- If you're comfortable, reveal something personal about yourself.
- Smile. Parrots will connect with this and take it as a sign that you're open.
- Make physical contact, whether through a pat on the shoulder, warm handshake, or a hug.
- Speak in superlatives, such as, "awesome," "extraordinary," and "the best."
- Begin an idea with "What if…" This invites a Parrot to freely explore their imagination.

Leadership Priorities:

- Enthusiasm: Motivates others through high optimism.
- Pioneering Spirit: Sees possibilities where others see obstacles.
- Relationship Focus: Invests in relationships that instill loyalty.
- Innovation: Resourceful problem solver.

Leadership Weaknesses:

- Reliability: Inconsistent attention to appointments and tasks.
- Process: Neglects the mechanics of how the operation will work.
- Impulsiveness: Quick to make decisions based on feelings rather than evidence.

- Follow-Through: Drawn to the beginnings of projects, not their completion.

Doves (S)

Doves, symbolized by the "S" in the DISC model, exude a calm presence and are deeply people-centric. Their harmonious nature draws others to them, making them invaluable team players. They're known for their unwavering loyalty, patience, and their attentive care in relationships.

When speaking to a Dove, phrases like "user-friendly," "thoughtful," and "holistic" resonate strongly with them. They appreciate predictability and thoroughness, seeking connections and meaningful interactions.

It's essential to approach them with patience and avoid pushing for immediate actions or diving into potential conflict situations; they thrive in stable, conflict-free environments.

Tips for Influencing a Dove:
- Be genuine.
- Slow down your pace.
- Hold gentle eye contact.
- Lower the intensity and volume of your voice.
- Take a sincere interest in their hobbies or family life.
- Body language should be relaxed rather than assertive.
- Focus on the positive impact their work has on others.
- Treat the Dove like a human being, not a cog in the machine.

Leadership Priorities:
- Trust: Skilled at earning personal loyalty.
- Thoroughness: Deliberate decision-making process.

- Customer Focus: Prioritizes customer needs.
- Inclusiveness: Builds consensus for major decisions.

Leadership Weaknesses:
- Passivity: May lack assertiveness required to address difficult issues.
- Risk Taking: May seek safety over necessary change.
- Conformity: May follow the pack instead of lead.
- Humility: May not display confidence and passion that inspires others.

Owls (C)

Owls, represented by the "C" in the DISC model, are methodical and prioritize tasks above all. Their detail-oriented nature ensures that every aspect is thoroughly examined, while their systematic approach guarantees structured and efficient results. These analytical thinkers often pose questions to get to the root of a matter.

They're attracted to terms like "meticulous," "organized," and "fact-checked," valuing precise, tailored solutions. To effectively communicate with an Owl, it's best to provide clear, fact-based information and avoid relying on gut feelings or vague assertions. They favor well-researched and organized ideas over randomness and mere intuition.

Tips for Influencing an Owl:
- Calm your voice.
- Be thoughtful in your speech.
- Give owls plenty of physical space.
- Give Owls extra time to fully consider decisions.
- When talking, de-emphasize feelings and stick to logic.

- Avoid saying, "I feel…" Instead, try, "I think…"
- Articulate the process you went through to arrive at your conclusion.
- Avoid too much eye contact. Intense eye contact is a form of aggression for this style.

Leadership Priorities:

- Rigor: Bases decision making on data and analysis.
- Knowledge: Skilled at explaining complex issues.
- Systematic Thinking: Strong commitment to building processes and procedures.
- Logical Decision Making: Utilizes data to arrive at conclusions.

Leadership Weaknesses:

- Low Energy: May lack needed enthusiasm to capture and inspire others.
- Lack of Connection: May fail to build a guiding coalition for major decisions.
- Minutiae: May fall into analysis paralysis.
- Hesitancy: May be risk averse when boldness is required.

Match The Moment, Not The Mirror

~Dan Silvert

Contrary to popular belief, the biggest reason we have unhealthy relationships isn't because we're surrounded by jerks who are out to get us. It's because we misunderstand our differences.

Our perceptions and reactions to situations are so ingrained that it takes conscious effort to see how another might respond differently to the same scenario.

To strengthen your relationships and collaborate more efficiently, remember this: **match the moment, not the mirror.**

Respect your peers' differences and lean in their direction. One of the most powerful applications of this framework is to understand others' underlying intentions and actions from a predictable style perspective.

By understanding the roots of others' behavior and adapting your own actions to match them, you can clear away their resistance. Collaboration and communication become easier.

Each of us possesses a distinct combination of Bird Styles—a primary and a secondary. Discovering your own might surprise you. Recognizing and embracing these styles is crucial for heightened self-awareness.

They highlight our natural strengths and areas that require growth, helping us harness our innate talents while also appreciating the unique strengths of those around us.

Reflect on your own dominant style:

- Are you the assertive Eagle?
- The lively Parrot?
- The compassionate Dove?
- Or perhaps the meticulous Owl?

By connecting with the DISC tool, you're not just understanding your abilities—you're unlocking your hidden genius.

Remember, the first step to being great is knowing yourself. Use the DISC to discover what you can do and set a clear path for growth.

Tool #4 Write Like an Amazonian

Amazon is (amongst many other things) known for its unique writing culture—they famously banned PowerPoint and forced everyone to write six-page memos for meetings. Writing the way they do is an incredibly powerful tool and we can learn A LOT from it.

In 2004, Bezos' passion for reading and writing inspired him to introduce a new structure at Amazon for presenting product and business development proposals. He mandated that all presentations be delivered in writing, conforming to several carefully developed frameworks.

Bezos' key argument for this unconventional approach is that, although written communication requires more time initially, it ultimately saves time due to the resulting clarity and the depth of thought necessary for written presentations. He claims that it's impossible to compose a six-page, narrative-structured memo without achieving clear thinking.

I've found the same to be true in project management, where complexity is everywhere.

Here's how you can apply Amazon's writing principles to project management, where clarity cuts through complexity.

1. Know Your Audience

The best writing feels like it was written *just for you*. As it turns out, that's exactly what great writers do.

Warren Buffet writes for his sister; Stephen King writes for his wife. Identify your reader:

- *Who are you writing for?*
- *What do they care about?*
- *How can you show that you're writing for them?*

Understanding your audience builds empathy and helps you recognize that not all writing warrants the same care and attention.

Spending an hour crafting the perfect email response is unnecessary if a straightforward, casual message will do just as good for your reader.

2. Structure for Skimmers

Most writing is never read (at least word-for-word). People have busy minds and default to skimming.

A reader should be able to grasp what you're saying and why just from skimming your document.

Use headings, bullet points, white space, and bold text to highlight key information, making your document easy to navigate.

3. Use Less Than 30 Words Per Sentence

Setting limits drives clear thinking and force the writer to use fewer words. Simple, brief explanations are usually understood better.

Short sentences improve readability and comprehension, crucial for unfamiliar readers. Stick to one idea per sentence and cut extra words for clearer, more impactful writing.

- Due to the fact that → because
- Totally lacked the ability to → could not

4. Be Objective: Replace Adjectives with Data

Adjectives are imprecise and don't contribute to making a decision. Specificity leads to clear results, rapid decision-making, and reduces confusion.

- Customers love Prime. → Customers with Prime spend on average three times more than those without, and we retain 90% of them y/y.
- Our project has a high user satisfaction → Our project has a 95% user satisfaction rate.
- This will make the endeavor extremely successful → This will increase output by 2.5%.

Quantify your statements. Data drives decisions, not vague descriptions.

Words such as "almost" and "significantly" should be eliminated as they create confusion. These words are imprecise, and no one knows exactly what they mean.

- Nearly all reports → 87% of reports
- Significantly better → +25 bonus points

6. Always Ask: Does Your Writing Pass the "So What?" Test?

No matter what the reasons are for communication, it should be for a purpose.

Readers should immediately know what action the presenter wants them to take and why it matters. If the action or takeaway isn't obvious, rethink your message.

Clearly state who needs to do what, why it's important, and when it needs to be done to avoid wasting time.

7. If You Get a Question, Reply with One of These Four Answers:

Jeff Bezos famously only allowed four different answers to a question at Amazon:

1. Yes
2. No.
3. A number.
4. I don't know, but I will know by X date.

If you're uncomfortable writing or saying option 4, you've got work to do.

8. Use Subject-Verb-Object Language

The goal of a presentation is to transfer thoughts to another person with as little confusion of the message as possible.

The simpler the sentences used, the more precisely the ideas will be translated.

- The budget was approved by the client. → The client approved the budget.

9. Avoid Cluttered Words and Phrases

Simplify your language. This makes your message more accessible.

Some examples of this that Bezos himself has put forward are:

- Utilize → use
- In order to → to
- Until such time as → until
- Due to the fact → because
- With the possible exception of → except
- Totally lacked the ability to → could not

10. Avoid Jargon and Acronyms

Ambiguity has no place in a project plan, email, or update.

Companies often use internal jargon, which can confuse new employees and external parties. Always explain an acronym the first time you use it.

- Explain "Critical Path Method (CPM)" the first time you use it.

I cannot overstate how important strong writing skills are. Leadership starts with successful communication. You cannot lead others if you cannot adequately share your thoughts and ideas with them.

Jordan B. Peterson put it best: *"If you can think, and speak, and write, you are absolutely deadly. Nothing can get in your way."* I wholeheartedly agree. Improving your writing also improves your thinking and speaking abilities.

To me, great writing focuses on:

- Clarifying your thoughts
- Simplifying the delegation process
- Making knowledge transfer easier
- Eliminating unnecessary meetings
- Supplying information for decision-making

I believe that over 70% of unnecessary meetings could be eliminated if the initiator were required to write a six-page memo following these frameworks.

Bezos himself is an exceptional writer, and I highly recommend reading all his shareholder letters. In my opinion, they serve as a masterclass in clear communication.

Chapter Takeaways

Here are the main takeaways for our chapter on becoming an effective communicator.

1. Project Managers need to be effective communicators because they are the ones leading their team to a desired outcome. It is their job to effectively communicate expectations, deadlines, and potential obstacles to their team.
2. Use the **Minto Pyramid Principle** by organizing communication hierarchically. Lead with the answer (your central message), then branch out into supporting ideas, and finally, end with the detailed data.
3. Remember to **prioritize and delegate** by using the acronym **CPQQRT:** set context, define purpose, describe quality and quantity, identify resources, and establish a timeframe. Implement a readback to verify that not only the content of your message was received, but the intent of the message was fully understood.
4. Use the **DISC** model to identify what your strengths and weaknesses are as a leader. Capitalize on your strengths. Grow in your weaknesses.
5. Embracing a culture of clear, written communication, by **writing like an Amazonian**. Doing so can streamline processes and influence your project outcomes.

Being a great communicator comes with patience and practice. Use the guide above to help you master this archetype.

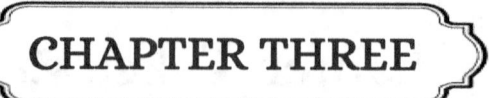

The Enforcer

Accountability is the glue that ties commitment to results.

~ Bob Proctor

I remember a senior project manager—*in title only*—who wanted and received the title when he hired on, but who was not qualified for the role. He knew how to manage budgets and was decent at handling paperwork, but he would not lead team meetings, mentor other managers, or communicate effectively.

He did not have control of the project and was not enforcing deadlines, safety standards, or quality guidelines. It became such a problem that the project executive met with him to resolve the issues.

During the meeting, he admitted he was incapable of filling the role of a senior project manager and asked for the title of project coordinator or document controller instead. His idea was that he could handle the paperwork and manage documents daily, while the assistants did the real work of communicating and collaborating with the trades. He was fired.

As a project leader, you cannot abdicate the responsibility of leading and holding others accountable.

Why Does a Project Manager Need to Be an Enforcer?

As a project manager, you're responsible for making sure *every* aspect of the job is done with excellence. That means checking in on the tasks you delegated to see that they're being done well.

Leading the project requires holding people accountable, and leading other project managers demands it. Being a project manager presupposes the ability to lead others and hold them accountable. If a project manager will not learn this, they will remain stuck in assistant or helper roles where they do tasks instead of leading people.

Without enforcing accountability, the goals will naturally disintegrate in the whirlwind of a project. Holding yourself and your team accountable will not only push them to work with absolute excellence, but it will also help them respect your authority and communicate to them where their boundaries are.

In this chapter, we'll discuss the main characteristics of the Enforcer, and three practices you can use to build this archetype: a culture of accountability, creating a compelling scoreboard, and using zero tolerance policies.

The Enforcer: Key Characteristics

"The Enforcer" is an archetype often used in stories, films, and video games. This character is typically a strong, disciplined individual who maintains order or enforces the rules set by a more powerful figure or organization.

They can be either a hero or a villain, depending on the narrative. They are known for their physical prowess, tenacity, and unwavering dedication to their duty, often placing the mission or the rules above their personal feelings or relationships. In other words, they're excellent at holding themselves and others accountable.

Everything good thrives in accountability. The project manager is the most accountable person on the project. When leaders are accountable, it inspires other leaders to exude the same traits.

Accountability is about the ownership of outcomes, which is critical to every project's and business' success. However, from my experience, I still see and hear about projects falling apart due to the absence of accountability.

Accountability does not mean a project manager must babysit, micromanage, or browbeat people to get things done. These tactics will often cause issues and animosity toward the project manager. Rather than being the only person holding people accountable, the enforcer empowers the entire team to uphold the project's accountability. Here are some of the main behavior patterns of The Enforcer.

Behavior Patterns of The Enforcer:

- You hold yourself to account, taking care where you give your word to do something, because when you do so, it really matters to you that you do it.
- Your mindset is that meeting the expectations you agreed to with others is a core value, both to you and the organization.
- You, therefore, take great care to get clarity of task and expectations.
- You know you are expected to interrogate any potential task to make sure you can do it.
- As soon as you know that you may not be able to do something that you said you would do, whether large or small, you take personal responsibility for both alerting the necessary people and finding solutions to the problem.
- You are timely, honest and direct in your conversations and expect the same from others. You believe that honesty is valued and appreciated, however challenging and uncomfortable, because it leads to richer learning, faster

problem solving, optimum results for the team and enterprise, and faster career development.

Enforcers hold themselves and others to the highest standards of execution. They aim to create win-win-win scenarios and hold people responsible for their actions to make it happen.

They carve out the path, turn the head lamp on, and lead everyone to success. **But everyone has to work for it.**

In order to help your team be responsible for their part of the job, let's take a look at accountability, responsibility, and how they each play a role in The Enforcer archetype.

Accountability vs. Responsibility

Think back to a time when seemingly small decisions impacted thousands of people. Situations have ended with decreased profits, lost time, or where things went completely wrong. In these situations, it's common to ask two questions:

1. Who was responsible?
2. Who should be held accountable?

Accountability and responsibility are often used interchangeably, but these words have distinct meanings that separate them and their roles in the workplace. It's imperative that leaders understand the difference if they want to move their organizations forward.

Although these two terms have some similarities, they can't be lumped into the same bucket.

Responsibility:

- Responsibility can be shared. You can work with a team of people to divide responsibilities.

- Responsibility is task-oriented. Every person on a team may be responsible for a given task that is required to complete a massive project.
- Responsibility focuses on defined roles, job descriptions, and processes that must be in place to achieve a goal.

Accountability:

- Accountability is something that can be specific to an individual depending on their skill set, role, or strengths.
- Accountability is what happens after a situation has occurred. It is how you respond and take ownership over the outcomes. Even during the most uncertain times, true leaders hold themselves accountable for the results.
- Accountability is committed to the successful completion of tasks assigned to you and being willing to take responsibility for everything that happens as a result of the actions that were taken.

Accountability breeds responsibility. Accountability in the workplace means that employees take responsibility for both their performance and business outcomes. Instead of playing the "blame game" when something goes wrong, they step up and take full ownership.

When the project manager is accountable for their decisions and actions, the project is more likely to be delivered effectively, on time, and in line with expectations. But, if there is no accountability, there's a high chance the project will fail to deliver all the intended outcomes.

Below are the three tools of The Accountability Partner to ensure your projects repeatedly stay on track for a successful completion. These are not actions you do once and forget about it. These are disciplines, which means they are continuous actions that take effort, thought, and intention.

Let's take a look at three tools to help you develop this architype.

Tool #1 Creating a Culture of Accountability

"Holding others accountable" has become a popular expression across the culture, but what does it really mean?

When a team member or leader accepts the obligation of achieving a specific outcome, they become accountable. By owning the result, they commit to perform and to achieve the desired end state. Accountability is the glue that ties commitment to the result.

Without team members and leaders who are accountable, projects would spin their wheels in the sand.

To prosper, leaders of the best projects and teams do everything they can to institute a culture of accountability. In a culture replete with accountability, every team member feels some ownership and responsibility for the larger results. More importantly, they feel accountable to each other.

When accountability pervades a culture, it isn't leaders who carry the strongest flame, but peers. Organizations that expect peers to engage openly and candidly about any and all performance unleash a tornado of personal responsibility.

When everyone knows they are expected to call others out when they observe any lack of commitment or sub-par performance, the entire organization of team members becomes accountable to each other.

Surprisingly to some, this doesn't produce a negative work climate or a highly confrontational atmosphere. Quite the opposite. When everyone is truly accountable to each other, relationships become deeply caring and get even stronger.

It is often said that great teams are made up of members who refuse to let each other down. This is exactly the case when it comes to creating a culture of accountability.

What is required to create such a workplace includes leaders who are, themselves, open and candid with each other. They then need to extend this expectation to each and every team member across the organization. They do this by inviting everyone to hold performance standards and a profound commitment to each other as the highest priorities. Nothing else can matter as much.

Once leaders demonstrate with their own actions that they will tolerate nothing less than frank and honest assessments of all performance, including their own, a culture of accountability has a great chance to emerge. For organizations, accountability and culture are destiny.

The only way you'll be able to ethically hold your team members accountable for meeting your expectations is to *set* clear expectations. Let's take a look at how project managers can communicate their expectations effectively.

Set Clear Expectations

Clarity is a crucial element in creating a culture of accountability. Employees need to know exactly what is expected in regard to performance and behavior, otherwise, they will certainly fall short.

Research shows that only 50% of employees are actually clear on what is expected of them.

What happens when expectations aren't clearly defined?

- **Disappointment.** Time is wasted and targets are missed because of confusion around expectations.
- **Distrust.** When things go wrong, blame is attributed and the performance improvement plans start to come out.
- **Disengagement.** People want to feel connected to a purpose. We want our jobs to matter. Clarity around expectations helps people stay connected and engaged to the mission.

The project leader does not let this happen on their projects. Take the lead by setting the expectations and communicating them effectively to the project teams. They do this by:

- **Outlining roles and responsibilities.** Take time to clearly define (or re-define) the role of each team member. This includes the specific responsibilities for each role which ensures that you have the right people and the right skills on the team to accomplish your team's mission.
- **Tracking milestones.** Publicly presenting milestones and the commitments that are associated with achieving those milestones. This includes publicly following up on those commitments made.
- **Highlighting the interconnections of tasks.** By showing team members how tasks relate to one another and how each team member needs to perform for the benefit of other team members, the project manager incentivizes team members holding one another accountable. If one team member cannot start a task until another team member finishes their task, the dependent team member has a vested interest in the other team member's success and will hold that team member accountable for timely and high-quality performance.

To make sure expectations are met, it is essential to confront poor performances early on. Keep reading to learn how to effectively confront team members who aren't acting with excellence.

Confront Poor Performance

Do you hold your people, trade partners, and vendors accountable to perform according to team goals? If the answer is no, it is likely you do not trust each other.

One of the key aspects of creating a culture of accountability is confronting poor performance. How do you help turn around problematic behavior? And how long do you let it go on before you cut your losses?

Addressing poor performance on your team is among the most unpleasant parts of a leader's role. As uncomfortable as it is, every leader needs the courage to have the difficult conversations. When you don't do this, you are often left with missing conversations.

Consider what's causing the problem. Sometimes, performance issues are unintentional and can be fixed with solid guidance, while other forms of poor work performance reflect deeper issues such as disengagement and how the employee feels about their job. The key is to be aware of where it might be coming from so you can best resolve it:

EXAMPLES	Unintentional	Intentional
Job-related	– Making mistakes – Missing deadlines – Mixing up instructions	– Neglecting instructions – Ignoring deadlines – Not responsive to feedback
Behavior-related	– Too loud – Over chatty – Accidentally late	– Rude to teammates – Disrespectful to management – Leaves early

Discussing a performance gap is much easier once clear expectations have been set. Regular communication is required to discuss their approach and process, to hold people accountable if expectations are being missed and to provide constructive feedback on performance to support their development.

Here is my five step framework you can use to help an under-performer:

1. Reflect

Ask yourself some reflective questions to see where you might be responsible. If you answer "Yes" to any of these questions, good for you for looking at yourself and being honest.

- Did I give them too much work?
- Were the targets we set unrealistic?
- Was I not clear enough in defining their role or their tasks?
- Was I not available to them when they needed my guidance?

2. Give a heads up and meet

Let the employee know you want to have a chat. Agree with them on a time and place. Do not take them by surprise.

3. Ask, Listen, & Be Specific

A good leader coaches. Attempt to find out if your employee is aware of their poor performance, and have them explain where they think it's coming from. Here are some conversation starters to probe these trickier subjects:

- "What's been going on that you feel might contribute to your performance?"
- "Do you feel any of my instructions were unclear?"
- "How have you been feeling at work recently?"

When it comes time to discuss your observations, don't give vague criticisms. Have specific, concrete employee feedback examples of poor performance to point out.

4. Create a Corrective Action Plan

This is best done collaboratively with the employee, so it feels like a solution rather than a punishment. Ensure it has measurable goals and timelines to mark their efforts to perform better. An action plan is not a vague promise to do better, but a clear laying-out of objectives.

Poor work performance action plan:

- Description of the problem: Be extremely clear and specific.
- Objectives to solve the problem: 1-3 goals for the employee.
- How progress will be assessed: How you'll measure improvement.
- Structured deadlines: The intervals that progress will be measured.
- Manager's role in the action plan: How you will support the employee.

5. Follow up

It may seem obvious, but unfortunately, many managers fail to follow up. Ask the person to check in with you regularly, or set up a time and date in the future to check progress.

It may be helpful to ask the employee if he has someone that he'd like you to include in the effort. A question that's been effective for: "Is there anyone you trust who can provide me with feedback about how well you're doing in making these changes?"

Following this framework sends a positive message: It says, "I want this to work, I want you to be successful, and I want you to feel comfortable; I got your back."

Of course, if the person makes positive changes, say so. Make clear that you're noticing the developments and reward them accordingly. You want a team that can make mistakes and learn from them.

In conclusion, the Enforcer makes accountability a non-negotiable by developing a culture of accountability. They establish an environment which produces the behaviors that allows for things to get done properly and enables people to develop.

As a result, all issues are dealt with efficiently and effectively; before they're ever allowed to escalate.

Another tool to help you hold your team accountable is creating a compelling scoreboard. Read the next section to learn how you can gamify excellence in your workplace.

Tool #2: Create a Compelling Scoreboard

This is the discipline of engagement. People and teams play differently when they are keeping score, and the right kind of scoreboards motivate the players to win.

The highest level of performance always comes from people who are emotionally engaged, and the highest level of engagement comes from knowing the score—that is, if people know whether they are winning or losing.

It must be simple—so simple that members of the team can determine instantly if they are winning or losing. Why does this matter? If the board isn't clear, the game you want people to play will be abandoned in the whirlwind of other activities. And if your team doesn't know if they are winning the game, they are probably on their way toward losing.

As an example, on my projects, my teams meet daily to review our project scoreboard which is on a mobile whiteboard we roll around the office.

The scoreboard includes a list of categories and deliverables that influence our project's critical flow and any other important outcomes we desire. Under each category are the associated tasks with the responsible team member. When a team member completes a promised commitment that moves us forward, it is tracked on the board.

It's a simple visual that illustrates the most important project goals and who on the team is supporting them. By looking at it, you will be able to tell who is contributing and who is not.

Take some time to think, play with, and set up your compelling scoreboard. Customize it until you find what is effective for your team and scope of work. Once you do, you will tap into an incredible amount of energy and engagement from your team that wasn't there before.

Gamifying excellence isn't the only way you can make sure your team is performing. If you're going to be in the top 1% of project managers, you're going to need to learn how to be firm when it comes to behaviors you don't want to tolerate. Check out tool #3 for tips on establishing a zero tolerance policy for behaviors that you don't want to see in the workplace.

Tool #3 Begin Using Zero Tolerance

The culture of any organization is shaped by the worst behavior the leader is willing to tolerate.

Zero tolerance systems on projects work everywhere we try them. The key is to not tolerate bad behaviors on your projects, and to keep people safe and making money. The following brief outline will demonstrate how this is most effectively done on projects.

The key is to establish common standards, orient everyone to the standards, and decide as a team on a collective form of consequences. After that, it works only if every member of the team is committed to implementing and enforcing the rules. For the first couple of days, people will be upset and you will have to remove people from the project. After that, everyone will get used to the system as long as you are consistent. After approximately six weeks of effort, and only then, will the teams begin to notice the difference in the outcomes and advocate for the system.

This applies to every component of your project: the cleanliness of the environment, the quality of communication, timeliness, notifications, meeting procedures, documentation quality, change management, scheduling, procurement, planning, safety—everything. Establish common standards and orient everyone to the standards.

What should we remember on every project?

Respect for people! That's it. That's why we do everything. We take care of the customer because we respect them, their staff, and their end users. We take care of our people because we respect them. We treat our trades and vendors well because we respect them. We are clean and organized because we respect people and their families. We bring materials on time, and just in time, because we respect other trades. We do not tolerate anything below standard because we respect people's lives, professional growth, and well-being of their families.

How do we do it?

- Everyone on the project must set the example and enforce the policy.
- The orientation should explain the approach to everyone.
- Daily huddles should remind people and train them on standards.
- If someone is observed, you say to them, "Because I care about your [X], we need to give you time to focus, re-train, or plan the work. So, let's have you go home for the day, and you can come back tomorrow for training."
- Send an e-mail to that person's company explaining why that person was allowed to go home. Ask for the person to be re-trained and offer for them to come back through orientation—if not a major violation.
- Log the name and violation on a log to track repeat offenders or folks who cannot come back.
- Hold the line, don't budget, be strict, calm trade partners, and in weeks the site will uphold the standard without a lot of oversight. Every new wave of contractors and people will have to be trained.

If you implement zero tolerance systems on-site, you can have a remarkably well-run project. You will have few safety incidents, higher quality of work throughout the project, and less fires to put out.

Chapter Takeaways

Here are the main takeaways for our chapter on becoming an effective enforcer.

- Project managers need to become effective enforcers in order to ensure their team is meeting expectations, acting with excellence, and doing their jobs well.
- Create a **culture of accountability** by setting clear expectations and addressing poor behavior.
- Create a **compelling scoreboard** to gamify the workplace. People perform better when they're competing.
- Implement **zero tolerance systems** to help hold performance standards throughout the project.

When the project manager masters the skillset of holding their team accountable in a respectful way, every team member reaps the benefits.

CHAPTER FOUR

The Builder

Build such a strong team that it's hard to tell who the boss is.

~ Unknown

I knew a senior-level project manager who had a huge gap in builder knowledge. I remember asking him a question about the drawings. He looked through a few, shrugged his shoulders, asked his assistant to find out, and announced he needed to walk the site. He didn't have builder experience and didn't know what he was doing.

The trades didn't like him because he would revert to yelling and bossing people around on-site. He set unrealistic expectations and offered no support. A few of the foremen even asked for him to be removed from the project. His lack of knowledge and poor leadership made the work environment toxic. Problems in the field would take forever to get resolved. Eventually, he was fired.

We need real builders who lean in to support our trades and last planners.

Why Does a Project Manager Need to Be a Great Builder?

People tend to think the role of a construction project manager is about pointing and directing. They're wrong. It's about knowing how to build, understanding the fundamentals, and being able to keep up with your trades in a coordination meeting. It is not about bossing people around and making random decisions.

The job of the superintendent is to drive the bus. The job of the project manager is to keep the lights green.

Project managers need to know how to do the work. If they don't, how can they help others achieve excellence? The more you as a project leader understand the fundamentals of construction, the more you are able to influence the path of the project and keep the lights green.

If you've never...

- Made a lift drawing from multiple sources, do you really know how to read drawings?
- Run a traverse, performed survey and layout tasks, or shot elevations, do you really know how to visualize things spatially?
- Had to create a model in Revit or another app, can you really translate drawings into a 3D image in your mind?

Every project manager should be able to do the following:

- Translate a 2D set of plans to a 3D image in their mind.
- Piece together details from multiple sources.
- Understand how building components come together.
- Be able to visualize elevations and a coordinate system.
- Visualize and piece things together to build.

In this chapter, we'll discuss the key characteristics of the builder archetype, and four tools you can implement in the workspace to help you build this skill: the eight wastes, The Last Planner System (LPS), constructability, and MEP systems.

Let's take a look at the primary characteristics of The Builder archetype.

The Builder

The "Builder" archetype is a term used in psychology and mythology to describe a personality type that is focused on creating, constructing, and making things.

People with this archetype are known for their practicality, resourcefulness, and problem-solving skills. They are driven by a need to build and create, and often have a natural talent for working with their hands.

In terms of personality psychology, the Builder archetype represents an individual's innate tendencies and motivations to create, construct, and make things.

Now how does this apply to construction project management?

Typically, every project team is coupled with a lead Project Manager and a lead Superintendent. The two act as business partners to manage the dials of project value and deliver a successful outcome.

The Builder is the archetype of the seasoned superintendent and the technical knowledge that comes from that background.

In order to be the best manager, you should understand and be able to interact with the work you are managing. This means exercising the builder archetype.

Modeling the Builder archetype will help project managers in the following ways:

- Be seen as the go-to industry expert
- Understand and remove constraints
- Communicate project updates and timelines
- Defend their schedule
- Quickly identify when someone isn't being honest
- Plan & coordinate the work with confidence

- Be able to see what's NOT on the drawings
- Communicate technical needs to stakeholders

Now that we've looked at the characteristics of the builder, it's time you know the real truth.

Project Managers Are Going to Kill Me.

Hear me out—this insight could put you in the top 1%.

Project managers or executives don't run construction projects, not like everyone is led to believe or the title implies. Generally speaking, they control the project's documentation, administration, and finances. All of which are important to the process and client relationship.

But they don't run the work. So, they don't run the job. The real driving force behind a project? The guys in the field.

This is why it's so important to embrace The Builder archetype.

Superintendents, their assistants, and trade partner foreman—these are the people who actually build the project. They direct the labor, which results in work-in-place, which results in payment.

The BEST PMs learn this quickly. They come to know and appreciate the difference between driving work-in-place and everything else that exists to enable it and support it.

"What we do for a living is drive work-in-place. That's what we get paid for and why we get paid at all. Everything else is supportive by definition." - Coty Fournier

This is one of the "aha" moments you uncover when you do this long enough and pay attention to see what's really going on.

Who cares about who outranks who and who is more important in the chain of command on a jobsite? Keep your ego in check.

Everyone   is   important.

Since work-in-place is WHY everyone gets paid, the guys who drive it have the most influence over the project. They do the thing we actually sell. They don't enable it or support it; they DO it.

When PMs embrace this reality and lead with it, their value skyrockets, making them indispensable to any project.

If you want to become The Influential Project Manager, then you must channel your inner builder.

Let's dive in and break down the qualities that make a first-class builder, so you too can model them.

Tool #1 The Eight Deadly Wastes

In the world of lean, waste is defined as anything that doesn't directly create value; waste can be thought of as the antithesis to value. Waste adds time and cost to your project.

There are 8 wastes in construction projects that every "builder" should know. A good way to memorize them is to use the acronym, DOWNTIME. They are as follows:

The 8 Wastes

1. **Defects:** Waste caused by rework, scrap, incorrect and/or insufficient information.
2. **Over/Under Production:** Waste caused by making more than is required or more than required right now.
3. **Waiting:** Waste caused by wasted time waiting for the next process step to occur.

4. **Non-utilized Talent:** Waste caused by failure to tap into the knowledge and expertise available in the organization.
5. **Transportation:** Waste caused by unnecessary movement of products and materials.
6. **Inventory:** Waste caused by products or materials sitting on the project site not being used or installed.
7. **Motion:** Waste caused by excess movement by people such as walking around and being on treasure hunts.
8. **Extra Processing:** Waste caused by working something over more than once or having waste in the value stream.

Once your eyes are opened to waste, it becomes an annoyance that is difficult to ignore. You, and everyone else, will be motivated to take incremental steps to remove the 8 wastes. You can begin a lead idea system, or a continuous improvement system to change the project for the better.

Now that we've discussed how you and your team can cut down waste, let's take a look at a specific system that will help you implement the builder archetype in your workday.

Tool #2 The Last Planner System

In the past few years of my career, I've been unlearning everything I thought I knew about construction management—because most of it simply isn't true.

Schedules tell you who does what by when, but nothing about "how." Over emphasis on administration—90% paperwork, 10% real data. The Critical Path Method and the Iron Triangle focus on the wrong things. All of it is designed to keep us stuck in a cycle of rush, push, and panic.

"In traditional design and construction projects, the level of follow-through on commitments made is unfortunately low. On average, only 54% of work planned for a given week is completed within the allotted schedule. As a result, the vast majority of projects are delivered late and over-budget, stakeholders end up not being satisfied with the end result, and workers suffer injuries on the job." - Lean Construction Institute

Instead, I've started embracing these simple truths:

1. Your projects don't rise to the level of your goals; they fall to the level of your systems.
2. Projects are production systems, and your data sets you free.
3. Speed comes from making work ready, not pushing.

All in an effort to reach a place where projects run smoother, faster, and with fewer headaches.

Design a production system, not a schedule.

Schedules are simply predictions of what should happen, and they do not account for variability. It must be understood that the schedule will change over the course of the project. The schedule is the demand that the production system answers.

The production system transforms inputs into reality and determines what will happen, and when it will happen.

If you're tired of the usual chaos and surprises that seem to come with every project, The Last Planner system is the solution you need. It embraces these three truths and will make you a stronger, more reliable builder.

What is the Last Planner System?

The Last Planner System® is a project management and production tool that is designed to improve collaboration and communication among construction teams. Think of the Last Planner System as the glue that holds your project together. But it's not just about sticking to a schedule—it's about making sure the work is done right, on time, and with fewer headaches.

At its core, LPS is all about getting the right people involved at the right time. Instead of top-down planning where the boss tells everyone what to do, LPS empowers those who are actually doing the work—the "last planners" like your superintendents, foremen, and crew leads. They're the ones who know what can realistically get done, so why not let them have a say in the planning?

Most construction projects don't fail because of bad intentions. They fail because of bad planning and poor communication. When everyone's working off different plans or assumptions, things go sideways fast. The Last Planner System fixes that by creating a plan, everyone can actually follow—because they helped create it.

The system helps you predict and avoid the usual pitfalls that derail projects, like missed deadlines, wasted resources, and frustrated teams. It's about improving workflow reliability—getting things done when you say they'll be done.

Using LPS isn't complicated, but it does require a shift in how you think about planning:

1. **Start with the end in mind**: Begin by setting clear project milestones. What needs to be done and by when? This is your "should" plan.
2. **Involve the team**: Get your crew leads and key players in a room. Together, work backward from those milestones to figure out what tasks need to happen and in what order. This is your "can" plan—what's realistically achievable.
3. **Make tasks ready**: Before a task gets the green light, make sure all the conditions for success are in place—materials,

information, and people. If something's missing, it's not ready to go.
4. **Commit to the plan**: Now that everyone's on the same page, commit to what will actually be done in the coming weeks. This is your "will" plan.
5. **Track and learn**: Finally, don't just set it and forget it. Track progress, learn from what goes wrong, and adjust as needed. This constant feedback loop is what makes LPS so powerful.

By adopting the Last Planner System, you'll see some real benefits:

- **Fewer surprises**: When everyone's on the same page, there's less room for unexpected issues to pop up.
- **Better teamwork**: When your team helps plan the work, they're more invested in getting it done right.
- **Improved efficiency**: With a clear plan and fewer delays, you'll use your resources more effectively.
- **Happier clients**: When you consistently deliver projects on time and within budget, your clients notice—and they keep coming back.

LPS has become one of the most popular tools used for production in the design and construction industry. Why?

Because it does a great job of connecting the many conversations that happen at different levels across time. The majority of the dissatisfactionand issues that happen on a project is a result of conversations that were never had or had with the wrong person at the wrong time.

From the project executive all the way down to the trade specific foreman—LPS is a collaborative planning process that involves all members of the project team.

The Rules of the Last Planner System

The Last Planner System (LPS) is all about clear, reliable planning. Here's how to nail it:

1. **Keep plans visible and updated**: Everyone should see the latest plan—no hiding or hoarding.
2. **Start with milestones**: Kick off with a high-level schedule. Focus on key dates and critical tasks.
3. **Detail plans as you go**: As deadlines approach, flesh out the specifics. The closer you get, the more detail you need.
4. **Collaborate with the doers**: The best plans come from the people who actually do the work. Get them involved early.
5. **Re-plan when necessary**: Things change. Adjust your plan to stay on track.
6. **Remove roadblocks together**: Identify and eliminate constraints as a team. Don't let obstacles fester.
7. **Prioritize reliability**: Reliable workflow means smoother operations. Focus on making sure tasks are ready and doable.
8. **Only commit to what's possible**: Don't start something you can't finish. Commit only to well-defined, sequenced, and properly sized tasks.
9. **Make and keep promises**: If you commit to something, deliver. And if you're unsure, speak up immediately.
10. **Learn from mistakes**: When things go wrong (and they will), dig into the why. Fix it for next time.
11. **Underload to ensure reliability**: Don't stretch your resources too thin. A little slack improves reliability.
12. **Focus on critical tasks**: Allocate your best resources to the most crucial tasks first.
13. **Keep a ready backlog**: Always have a list of ready-to-go tasks to prevent downtime and delays.

If you follow these rules, you'll create a project environment where everyone knows what's happening, when it's happening, and how it's going to get done. Now that you have a system to build trust, improve efficiency, and deliver projects on time, let's get down to the nuts and bolts of mechanical, electrical, and plumbing systems that you as a builder need to know.

Tool #3 A Beginner's Guide to Understand MEP

Mechanical, Electrical, & Plumbing (MEP) systems encompass the components that make a building livable and functional. They include heating, ventilation, and air conditioning (HVAC), lighting, power systems, fire systems, and plumbing services.

MEP can constitute up to 60% of the total construction expense, making them a significant part of the budget. Understanding it isn't just useful, it's a career game-changer. With this knowledge, you'll be better equipped to influence the construction process, solve problems that arise, and deliver a project that meets the needs of its users.

My goal in this section is to break down the complexities of MEP systems into easy-to-understand sections. We'll cover what these systems are, why they're important, and how they fit and work together in a building project.

These components are fundamental to making any building work effectively and comfortably. However, they often present a challenge even to seasoned professionals in construction.

Why should you learn about MEP? Because it's one of those "high-value skills." Master it, and you'll stand out in the AEC field, opening doors to exciting opportunities.

The goal here is simple—to break down these complexities and provide you with a clear understanding of MEP systems. We'll take a close look at what they are, why they're crucial, where they fit into the overall construction process, and how they work together to create a well-functioning building.

After finishing this guide, you'll have a solid understanding of the basics of MEP. With this knowledge, you'll be better equipped to influence the construction process, solve problems that arise, and deliver a project that meets the needs of its users.

MEP - What Are The Scopes?

1. **Mechanical:**
    a. Heating, Ventilation, & Cooling (HVAC)
    b. Building Management Systems (BMS)
2. **Electrical:**
    a. Power & Lighting
3. **Plumbing:**
    a. Water, Drainage, Gases
4. **Also Includes:**
    a. Fire Protection
    b. Low Voltage Systems

Think of a building as a human body. The MEP systems are the vital organs that keep it alive and functioning:

- The **Mechanical** systems (HVAC) are the lungs, managing airflow.
- **Electrical** systems act like the nerves, powering the building.

- **Plumbing** mirrors the circulatory system, moving water around.

- And **Fire Protection?** That's the immune system, keeping the building safe.

They all work together, making the building functional and comfortable.

Why Every Project Manager Should Understand MEP Systems:

- Up to 60% of your project's budget could be tied up in MEP. That's a huge chunk of change you need to manage wisely.

- The planning and execution of civil, structural, and architectural (CSA) components on a site are directly influenced by the positioning and distribution of MEP equipment.

- MEP changes are common and can throw a wrench in the works for other teams. Knowing MEP helps you stay one step ahead.

- The procurement, initiation, testing, and commissioning of equipment can influence your schedule. Understanding these systems helps you plan and prevent delays.

- Without a solid MEP understanding, you'll be leaning on others for decisions about scheduling, scope changes, and budgeting. And that's not where you want to be.

Let's begin.

1. Mechanical Systems

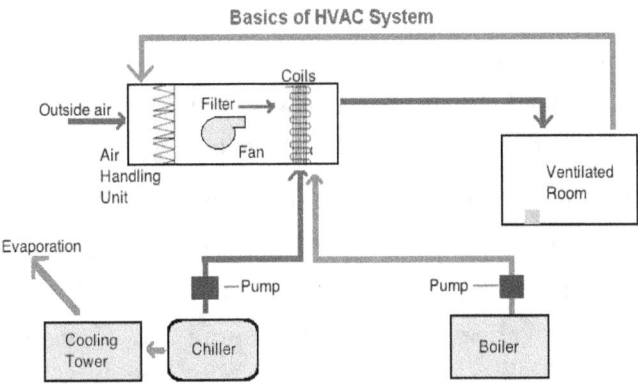

Mechanical systems in a building encompass all systems designed to control climate and maintain air quality. They are responsible for heating, cooling, and ventilating spaces, ensuring a comfortable and healthy environment for occupants.

Heating Systems:

These systems warm up a building. There are many ways to generate heat, such as using gas, electricity, or even recovering heat from other sources. They can be local (like a radiator in a room) or central (like a big boiler in the basement).

- *Heating Hot Water:* The process begins with the boiler, where water is heated to a high temperature. This boiler uses a fuel source, such as gas or oil, to heat the water.
- *Pump:* A circulating pump then moves the heated water from the boiler to various parts of the building.
- *Heat Exchanger/Coils:* These pipes run through a heat exchanger, which in many systems is a coil located inside an Air Handling Unit (AHU) or a Fan Coil Unit (FCU). The heat exchanger or coil is where the hot water's heat is

transferred to the air, which is then distributed throughout the duct system.

- *Return Path:* After releasing its heat to the air, the now cooler water returns back to the boiler through a separate set of pipes. The water is reheated, and the cycle begins again.
- *Thermostat:* Throughout this process, a thermostat measures the temperature of the room's air. If the room's temperature drops below the set point on the thermostat, it sends a signal to the boiler and the pump to start heating and circulating water again.

Cooling Systems:

These systems remove heat to cool down a building. They use different methods like chilling water or evaporating it to cool down the air. They can be small units in each room or big ones that cool the whole building.

- *Chilled Water:* At the heart of this system is a machine called the chiller. The chiller has a refrigeration cycle that cools down water. This process involves using a refrigerant, which changes from a gas to a liquid and back again. When the refrigerant turns from a liquid into a gas in the chiller's evaporator, it absorbs heat from the water. This process cools down the water drastically, usually to around 45 degrees Fahrenheit.
- *Pump:* Once the water is chilled, a pump pushes the chilled water out of the chiller and towards the cooling coils located in air handlers or fan coil units throughout the building.
- *Cooling Coils:* The chilled water flows through these coils. As room air is forced over these coils by a fan, the air absorbs the coolness from the chilled water. As a result, the air cools

down and is then distributed throughout the building, thereby reducing the indoor temperature.

- *Return Path:* After the water circulates through the system and transfers its cold energy to the air, it warms up. The now warmer water returns back to the chiller to start the process again.

Ventilation Systems

Ventilation is all about controlling air movement. It gets rid of stuffy air, controls humidity, and provides fresh air. It can be as simple as opening a window or as complex as a system with fans, ducts, and filters.

- **Air Handlers:** These are large metal units that condition and circulate air as part of the HVAC system. It's designed to be durable and to protect these elements from the elements and various environmental conditions. These elements include:
  - *Fan:* This is the heart of the system. It pushes air around, and its speed can be adjusted to control airflow.
  - *Filters:* These clean the air by trapping particles like dust and pollen. To keep the air fresh, filters need to be cleaned or replaced regularly.
  - *Heating and Cooling Coils:* These change the air temperature. Heating coils warm the air, and cooling coils cool it down.
  - *Humidifier:* This part adds moisture to the air, usually during dry months.
  - *Dampers:* These are like valves that control how much air goes to different parts of the building. In high-tech systems, they're usually adjusted automatically.

- *Mixing Box:* This is where the system decides how much fresh outdoor air to mix with the air already inside the building.
- *Controls:* This is where you make adjustments, like changing the temperature or fan speed.
- *Motor:* This powers the fan that moves the air around.
- *Belt and Sheave (pulley):* The belt connects the motor to the fan, and the sheave controls the fan speed.

- **Fan Coil Units (FCU) & Variable Air Volume (VAV) Boxes:** These units heat or cool the air moving through a duct system.

- **Exhaust Systems:** These systems remove air from inside the building.

Building Management System (BMS)

The Building Management System (BMS) is the brain that controls these systems. It can adjust temperature, turn systems on or off, and even talk to other building systems.

- *Automated Control:* The BMS uses Direct Digital Control (DDC) and Programmable Logic Controllers (PLC) to automate and manage the building's functions. This means it can turn systems on or off, adjust temperatures, or control lighting based on pre-set criteria or schedules.

- *Communication:* The BMS is not an isolated system. It communicates with other systems in the building. For example, it might adjust the HVAC system based on information from a security system that tells it how many people are in the building.

- *Remote Management:* One major advantage of a BMS is its ability to be controlled remotely. This means a facilities manager can adjust building systems from a computer, without having to manually adjust each system.

2. Electrical Systems

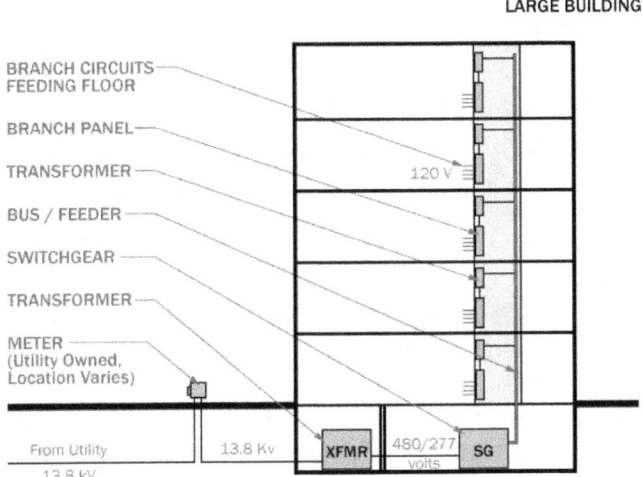

Electrical systems in a building include power distribution, lighting, fire alarm systems, and security systems. They power our lights, appliances, and technology, making our buildings functional, safe, and comfortable. Here are the main components:

- *Supply*: Buildings receive electricity from a utility company through primary service lines.
- *Distribution*: Once inside, electrical panels distribute this power throughout the building via circuits.
- *Regulation*: Devices like circuit breakers and fuses protect the system from overloads or short circuits.

How Does a Building Get its Power?

Imagine power going on a journey from its source to the light switch in a room. Here's how that journey looks:

Step 1: Power Generation & Transmission

First, electricity is created at a power station. There are many ways to do this—using coal, natural gas, water, wind, or even the sun.

Once the electricity is created, it's sent far and wide through a network of high-voltage lines called the electrical grid.

Step 2: Power Distribution

Before the electricity can be used in a building, it needs to be at a safe voltage level. This is done at a substation, where devices called transformers reduce the voltage. The levels depend on the type of building—for houses, it's typically 120/240 volts, and for larger commercial buildings, it's usually 277/480 volts.

Step 3: Power Enters the Building

From here, the electricity goes to the building through service lines. There's an electrical meter that measures how much electricity is used for billing purposes. The service line then connects to the main electrical panel in the building.

Step 4: Power Distribution Within the Building

Inside the main electrical panel, the power is divided into smaller parts called circuits. Each circuit is protected by a circuit breaker, which can switch off the circuit if too much electricity flows at once.

Sub-panels are smaller service panels that distribute electricity to a specific area of a building, such as a garage, home addition, or a specific floor in a large building. They are connected to the main breaker panel and are often used when the main panel doesn't have enough space for additional circuits.

Step 5: Power Reaches Its End Use

The circuits run all around the building to reach the places where electricity is needed, like outlets, lights, and appliances. When you flip a switch or plug something in, electricity flows to it, and it turns on or starts working.

3. Plumbing Systems

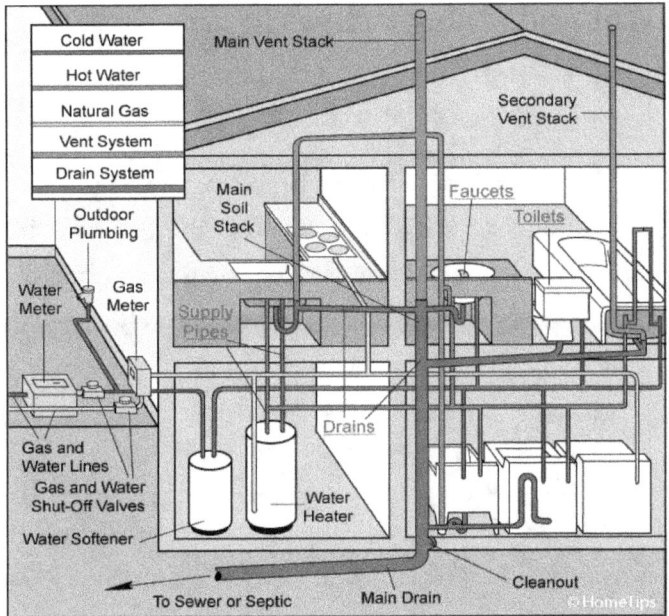

Plumbing systems are all about water. They make sure clean water comes into a building and waste water goes out.

Plumbing follows the basic laws of nature—gravity, pressure and water seeking its own level.

- *Water Supply:* This is the system that brings in fresh water. It's used for drinking, cooking, washing—all the things we need clean water for.

- *Drain-Waste-Vent (DWV) System:* This system takes care of the dirty work. It removes wastewater and waste from the building. It also ensures unpleasant sewer gases are sent outside, not inside.

- *Fixture Traps:* These are shaped like a "U" and have a critical job. They hold a little water, which forms a barrier that stops sewer gases from coming back into the building.

How Does Hot and Cold Water Move Throughout a Building?

Step 1: Water Supply

Buildings receive their water supply from a municipal water line or a well. This water is generally cold. When it enters the building, it's directed to two different systems—one for cold water, and one for hot. The cold water is ready to be distributed immediately to sinks, toilets, and outdoor faucets.

Step 2: Heating the Water

For the hot water supply, the cold water first needs to be heated. It's directed to a water heater or boiler that can be powered by electricity, gas, or even solar power. The heater warms up the water to a set temperature and then sends it to the hot water lines.

Step 3: Distribution

Both hot and cold water lines run throughout the building, typically within the walls, floors, or ceilings. They branch off to provide water to individual fixtures like sinks, showers, and washing machines.

When a hot or cold water tap is turned on, water pressure pushes the water out of the faucet, ready for use. The temperature can be adjusted at the tap by mixing hot and cold water as required.

It's important to note that the hot water lines are insulated to keep the water hot and to save energy. Also, to ensure a continuous supply of hot water, the water heater maintains the water temperature even when no hot water is being used.

The entire process is a simple but clever use of pressure and gravity to move water around the building.

4. Fire Protection Systems

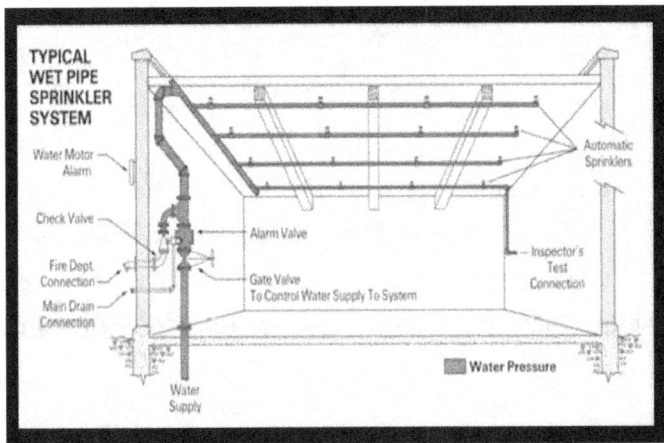

Fire protection systems are crucial in every building. They serve to detect fires early, control their spread, and ultimately extinguish them, safeguarding both lives and property. Here are the key components:

Fire Detection:

The first line of defense is early detection. This system includes smoke detectors, heat detectors, and fire alarm control panels.

Fire alarms work by constantly monitoring the environment for signs of fire, such as smoke or excessive heat. When these signals are detected, the system triggers an alarm to warn occupants.

The alarm system is also typically connected to a central monitoring station or directly to local fire departments, alerting them to the situation.

Fire Suppression:

Once a fire is detected, we need to stop it from spreading. This is where fire extinguishers and automatic sprinkler systems come into play.

Fire sprinklers are typically ceiling-mounted and connected to a network of pipes that are filled with water. Each sprinkler head contains a heat-sensitive element, such as a glass bulb filled with a glycerin-based liquid.

When the temperature around the sprinkler head reaches a certain threshold (typically 135-165 degrees Fahrenheit), the heat-sensitive element bursts, activating the sprinkler. Water is then discharged onto the fire below, suppressing or extinguishing the fire and preventing it from spreading.

Evacuation:

These systems support safe evacuation from the building in case of a fire. They include emergency lighting to illuminate exit paths, and clearly marked exit signs.

How Do These Systems Relate to Each Other?

Understanding how MEP systems work together is essential for smooth construction management. Here's a quick breakdown:

1. **Mechanical and Electrical:** All our heating, ventilation, and cooling equipment need electricity to run. So, we need to plan our electrical system to power our mechanical systems correctly.

2. **Mechanical and Plumbing:** Our ductwork (for heating and cooling) and pipework (for water) often occupy the same spaces in a building. This means we need to carefully plan their routes to avoid them clashing, and make sure we can still access everything for future repairs.

3. **Electrical and Plumbing:** Electricity and water don't mix well! We must keep electrical and plumbing systems safely apart to avoid risks if any leaks happen.
4. **Fire Protection:** When planning our MEP systems, we always have to think about fire safety. This can affect the materials we use, where we put things, and how our systems work during emergencies.

Understanding these relationships allows construction managers to foresee potential conflicts and streamline the installation process. The goal is to have these systems operate cohesively for the lifespan of the building, providing comfort and safety to its occupants.

MEP Documentation

MEP documentation is a vital part of construction, detailing all the essential system designs and guidelines. It includes various reports, drawings, and specifications that cover everything from design to installation and maintenance.

Together, these documents ensure that everyone involved in the design, construction, and maintenance of the building understands the MEP systems, how to install them, and how to keep them working efficiently for years to come.

Reports:

- **Basis of Design (BOD):** This document outlines the design principles, requirements, and applicable codes or standards that the design needs to meet.
- **Short Circuit Analysis / Arc Flash:** This is a study conducted to determine the magnitude of current flowing throughout an electrical system during a short circuit or an electrical fault.

- **Test and Balance (TAB):** This is a report showing that HVAC systems have been tested and adjusted to deliver optimal performance and comfort.
- **Commissioning (Cx):** This is a quality assurance process to verify that building systems are designed, installed, tested, and capable of being operated and maintained as per the owner's project requirements.
- **Day-lighting Analysis:** This is an evaluation of the amount of natural light in a building to enhance energy efficiency and occupant comfort.
- **Energy Efficiency Reports:** These reports assess the energy performance of the building's systems, outlining measures to improve efficiency.
- **Load Calculations Report:** This report contains the calculation of heating and cooling loads for each space in a building, critical for sizing HVAC systems.

Drawings:

- **Floor Plans:** These are scale diagrams of the arrangement of rooms in the building from above, showing how spaces are connected.
- **Enlarged Plans:** These are detailed, zoomed-in versions of certain sections of floor plans, highlighting specific areas or elements.
- **Diagrams (single line, riser, flow, controls):** These are simplified drawings that illustrate the components and functionality of electrical and mechanical systems.
- **Details:** These drawings provide extra information, in-depth specifics, or close-ups about a particular part of the building or system.

- **Schedules:** These are detailed charts that list various elements and their details for reference and coordination.
- **Layouts for Equipment Rooms:** These drawings show the physical arrangement and location of equipment in specific rooms.
- **Sections and Elevations of Critical Areas:** These drawings show a vertical 'cut-through' view of the building, showing structure and component heights.
- **MEP Coordination Drawings:** These show all building services (mechanical, electrical, and plumbing) in one drawing to coordinate their location and avoid clashes.
- **Shop Drawings:** These are detailed, 'pre-manufacture' drawings typically produced by the contractor, manufacturer, or fabricator.

Specifications:

- **Quality Assurance and Quality Control (QA/QC) Requirements:** These are guidelines and procedures to ensure the project will meet the required standards of quality.
- **Maintenance Requirements:** These are the necessary tasks, frequencies, and standards to maintain the building systems over time.
- **Warranty Information:** These are the terms and conditions that outline what is covered by the manufacturer if a system or component fails.
- **Material and Equipment Standards:** These are specifications that describe the quality and performance characteristics of materials and equipment used.
- **Installation Standards and Requirements:** These are guidelines and procedures for how systems and components should be installed.

- **Start-Up, Testing, and Cx Requirements and Documentation:** These outline the processes for initializing systems, testing their operation, and documenting their compliance with design intentions.
- **As-Built Documentation:** This includes any modifications or field changes to the original design that occur during the construction process.
- **Operation and Maintenance Manuals:** These are detailed guides that outline how to operate and maintain the systems installed.

Final Takeaways on MEP Systems

In conclusion, understanding MEP systems is key for influential construction project management.

When you understand how these systems function, interact, and require maintenance, you'll be better equipped to manage the construction process, solve problems that arise, and deliver a project that meets the needs of its users.

While these systems may seem complex, breaking them down into their essential components and functions can make them much more approachable and manageable.

It's all about taking one step at a time and building on your knowledge as you grow in your role.

Chapter Takeaways

Here are the main takeaways for our chapter on becoming an effective builder.

- It is essential for a project manager to become a great builder so they can ensure the job is being done right.
- Memorize the **Eight Deadly wastes** to identify and remove waste on your jobsite for better schedule and safety outcomes.
- Use **The Last Planner System** to cut waste and put systems in place for more reliable and predictable workflow.
- Learn **MEP systems** so you have the knowledge base to make the right decisions for each construction project.

Becoming a great builder is essential to helping your team build great projects. By implementing these tools, you'll enable your team to work with absolute excellence.

CHAPTER FIVE

The Leader

Build such a strong team that it's hard to tell who the boss is.

~ Unknown

When I was leading a project for a healthcare organization, I was in charge of the most important project they had.

The stakes were high. A donor had given the largest donation in the organization's history to fund this project, and they promised it would be delivered on time. The pressure was intense, not just from the donor but from everyone in the organization. I could feel the weight of responsibility every time I walked onto the site.

As the project progressed, I noticed morale was dropping. The team was stressed, and it started to show in their work and attitudes. We were nearing burnout, and the project was beginning to struggle. I knew something had to change.

This experience taught me that leadership isn't just about managing tasks; it's about inspiring and supporting the people you lead. It's about creating an environment where everyone feels valued and motivated. I often thought back to this project, especially when I faced tight deadlines or when my team was struggling. The memory of a junior project engineer, nervous but hopeful, sharing his idea with the team, reminded me of the power of encouragement.

Things changed when that project engineer approached me with a suggestion to streamline our work. He was hesitant, unsure if his idea would be taken seriously, but I encouraged him to share it. His idea turned out to be a game-changer—productivity improved and it really helped the project. The mood on-site lifted. The team found new purpose, and everyone felt their input mattered.

At that moment, I realized leadership is about helping others step up and lead alongside you.

The transformation was clear when I saw my team working with renewed energy and commitment. The stress and fatigue that once held us back were replaced with drive and determination. We finished the project not just on time, but with pride in what we achieved together. We became a strong, united team, each person giving their best and supporting one another.

This story matters because it shows that true leadership isn't about being in charge; it's about lifting others up and helping them reach their full potential. The greatest success comes not from what you do alone, but from what you inspire your team to do together.

If I could summarize this story in one sentence for the reader to end with, it would be: **Leadership is the solution to all your problems.**

All problems are, fundamentally, leadership problems. And the good news is that leadership is the solution to every problem. Every single problem.

Why a Project Manager Needs to Be a Great Leader

When you're the project manager on the job, you're the one leading the team. Your job is to build people into remarkable performers, to build these performers into amazing teams, who then build high-quality, profitable projects. Note that people and teamwork come before the work or the money.

If you struggle to lead in the project management space, then there is a very good chance that your projects will be over budget and behind schedule.

Being a leader isn't just about organizing tasks and telling people what to do. It's about showing passion, enthusiasm, and expertise to inspire your team to be the best they can be.

In this chapter, we'll discuss the key characteristics of a leader, and several tools to help you build this skill set in the workplace: creating a culture of extreme ownership, being the captain your team needs, developing emotional intelligence, and learning how to influence people, and becoming the eye of the storm.

Let's take a look at the key characteristics of a great leader.

The Leader: Key Characteristics

The "Leader" archetype is a term used in psychology and mythology to describe a personality type that is characterized by their drive to guide, direct, and influence others. Leaders are driven by a strong sense of purpose and vision, and they have the charisma to inspire those around them.

The goal of leadership seems simple: to get people to do what they need to do to support the mission and the team. But the practice of leadership is different for everyone. There are nuances to leadership that everyone has to uncover for themselves.

Let's explore how you can embody The Leader archetype and guide your team to success.

Driven

Project leaders possess an unrelenting need for achievement and constant self-improvement. They are highly motivated, set ambitious goals for themselves, and continually push their limits to accomplish more. Their drive is a fundamental force that propels them to excel in their respective domains.

Humble

Humility in leaders is characterized by self-confidence in one's ability while understanding that there's always room for improvement and that others' experiences and knowledge are valuable. They recognize their strengths and weaknesses and are willing to learn from others, regardless of rank or position.

Integrity

Leaders maintain a strong moral compass, adhering to not only what is legal but also what is right. They act ethically and responsibly, earning the trust and respect of their peers and colleagues. This trait builds a positive work environment and leads to long-term success.

Empathetic

Great leaders understand and value the emotions and perspectives of their team members. By creating a supportive environment where everyone feels heard and respected, you naturally increase collaboration and job satisfaction, leading to project success.

Decisive

Leaders must make strong decisions, weighing the pros and cons and choosing the best course of action. By being decisive, you navigate challenges and drive your project forward.

Resilient

Resilient leaders maintain a positive attitude in the face of challenges, using setbacks as opportunities to grow. This resilience inspires your team to persevere and ensures the project stays on track.

Adaptable

Adaptable leaders adjust plans and strategies as needed, maintaining team morale and keeping the project on track. Flexibility is crucial for success in complex, unpredictable environments.

Inspirational

Inspirational leaders motivate their teams to take on challenges and strive for excellence. By celebrating achievements and providing constructive feedback, you create a high-performance culture that drives project success.

Accountable

Accountable leaders take ownership of their actions and the project's outcomes. By establishing clear expectations and following through on commitments, you build trust with your team and stakeholders, ensuring everyone stays focused on the project's goals.

Now that you know what a great leader looks like, it's time to understand the 4 stages of team development.the 4 stages of team development

The 4 Stages Of Team Development

Let's take 2 Project Managers:

One has a detailed plan, the latest AI tools, and takes full control.

The other has a clear purpose, a cohesive team, and empowers others.

Who would you put your money on?

Let me tell you about a mistake I made early in my career.

I thought having the perfect plan and the best tools was the key to success. I was managing a major healthcare project with all the right tech, but something was off. My team wasn't clicking and it showed in our outcomes.

There was tension, constant confusion, and constant delays. Despite the tools and plans, the project stalled. The problem? Poor team dynamics. No trust.

What I learned was simple but powerful: No amount of Gantt charts, ConTech, or spreadsheets can replace a strong, cohesive team.

Team first, technicalities second.

That's why my money is on the project manager who focuses on the people, not just the plan.

Why Building a Strong Team is Critical

If you don't focus on team development, here's what happens: communication breaks down, conflicts arise, and the everyone begins to panic.

You can plan a project according to all the best practices in the world, engineer a flawless production plan for your project, and STILL fail miserably if your team is not healthy and high functioning.

Few teams hit the ground running as high performing. Most go through a multi-stage development process, known as the Tuckman model, which breaks down into four stages:

1. Forming
2. Storming
3. Norming
4. Performing

Master these stages, and your team will thrive. Skip them, and you'll face endless friction. Let's dive in.

Phase 1 – Forming

Get to know each other.

The first stage is forming. Here, everyone is getting to know each other. There's excitement, but people are unsure of their roles. Everyone's being polite and typically no one intentionally ruffles feathers.

If you skip this phase, team members may struggle with unclear roles and poor communication.

- Clearly define roles and responsibilities.
- Perform personality profiles to understand each other's strengths.
- Start building clear communication pathways early.

Laying this foundation will build trust and set the stage for success.

Phase 2 – Storming

Handle conflict head-on.

As the project moves forward, the team hits the storming phase. Here, conflicts arise as people's working styles clash. The team will begin stepping on each other's toes.

Again, it may be nothing intentional, but feelings are going to get hurt, someone's nose is going to get out of joint. Team members are learning about each other. It's natural and necessary for growth.

If you avoid conflict, the team may become disengaged or frustrated. Instead, guide your team through the storm by addressing conflict head-on.

- Encourage open discussions and healthy conflict.
- Create a safe space where people can speak up without fear.
- Praise team members for bringing up tough issues.

Your team will never develop if you do not lead them through the storming phase. There is no going around.

Embrace this phase, and you'll come out stronger.

Phase 3 – Norming

Establish routines and systems.

Once conflicts are resolved, your team enters the norming phase. Roles are clearer, and the team begins working more effectively together.

But without established systems, the team can still struggle.

- Begin grading team health.
- Normalize regular meetings with clear agendas.

- Implement consistent communication systems.
- Create standards and accountability structures that keep everyone on track.

At this point the leader is crucial to the success of the team. This is where your team starts to find its groove and prepares for high performance.

Phase 4 – Performing

Achieve peak performance.

In this stage, your team is fully in sync. Everyone knows their role, and they're using their strengths to drive the project forward. The leader takes a step back, and the team runs like a well-oiled machine. The team is so strong, it's hard to tell who the boss is.

Without reaching this stage, your project will never run as smoothly as it could. To get here, focus on trust and empowering your team.

- Celebrate wins as a team.
- Delegate responsibilities and trust your team to deliver.
- Continue encouraging open communication and feedback.

This is where we want our teams to be. When your team hits this phase, your project will soar. You'll see a team that gives a lot, spends **time with each other,** and isn't afraid to be **open and vulnerable.**

Keep Moving Forward

STAGES OF TEAM FORMATION

[Diagram showing performance over time through Forming Stage, Storming Stage, Normal Stage, and Perform Stage, with Reset arrows indicating setbacks can return the team to earlier phases. Points A and B are marked along the progression.]

Occasionally, setbacks will throw your team back into earlier phases. That's normal. What's important is to guide your team through each stage until they reach peak performance.

By following these steps, you can avoid the same mistake I made. Don't just rely on tools and plans—invest in your team's development, and your projects will thrive.

It's All on You, but Not about You.

Leadership is all on you, but it's not about you. It's about the team. The moment you put your interests above the team is the moment you fail as a leader.

Use these strategies and tactics with the goal of helping others and accomplishing the team's mission. If the team succeeds, you win as a leader and as a person. But more importantly, your people win. That is true leadership.

Let's look at some tools that will help you become the leader you were meant to be.

Tool #1 Creating a Culture of Extreme Ownership

To lead a team is to take ownership. To lead a team well requires extreme ownership—a term made popular by Jocko Willink and Leif Babin, the authors and Navy SEALs behind the New York Times best-selling book leadership book *Extreme Ownership*.

It is defined as *"The leader must own everything in his or her world. There is no one else to blame. ...The best leaders don't just take responsibility for their job. They take Extreme Ownership of everything that impacts their mission."*

It's the practice of taking responsibility for everything in your world: your actions and decisions, the actions and decisions of your team, as well as factors that you don't control directly but that affect the overall strategic goals you are setting out to achieve.

The best way to introduce, develop, and maintain a culture of Extreme Ownership with your team is to model it.

When your people arrive at work, they will see how you lead, and over time, they will mirror it. When you take Extreme Ownership, your team will take Extreme Ownership. When you make excuses and blame others, your team will make excuses and blame others. That's how leadership works.

Culture change doesn't happen overnight. But as you continue to implement the Extreme Ownership mindset and use the Laws of Combat to ensure your team's success, you will see a transformation.

If you want people to take ownership, you must give them ownership.

Give your new people responsibility, let them lead projects, present briefs to leadership, run meetings, and everything else you do.

When things go well, give your people the credit. This will encourage them to take more ownership over other aspects and reward them for a job well done. When things don't go well, you must take responsibility as their leader and continue to train them. This ownership shows recruits that mistakes aren't the end of the world if they take ownership and learn from them. When your people see how successful they and the team are, they will maintain the culture even after you're gone.

As a leader, you are responsible for creating a Culture of Extreme Ownership. If you exemplify these leadership principles, your people will see the value of this culture. Model it, and others will begin to follow your lead.

Think of yourself as more than a leader. You don't just manage projects. You're the captain of your project's ship, and unless you're doing your job well, you and your entire crew are liable to sink.

Tool #2 Be the Captain Your Team Needs

The heart of great teams isn't the stars, the coaches, or the money. It's the captain—an unconventional leader who puts the team first.

The Captain's Role:

Sam Walker's research in "The Captain Class" identified 17 legendary sports teams. The common thread? **Captains who were relentless, selfless, and courageous.** They tackled tough tasks, made difficult decisions, and always prioritized the team over personal glory.

One example: Wayne "Buck" Shelford of the All Blacks, who inspired such loyalty that teammates would "walk over broken glass" for him. This quality—leading by example—glued teams together and propelled them to greatness.

Walker's insights change how we see leadership. High-performing teams don't need superstars; they need dedicated leaders who think of the team first. This is a blueprint for building any successful team, on or off the field.

Be The Captain Your Team Needs

Alex Ferguson, the legendary Manchester United manager, echoed this idea. Once the game starts, it's the captain, not the coach, who ensures the team acts as one. In project management, you are that captain. You translate goals into action and ensure your team meets objectives.

But great leaders aren't always who you'd expect. They're not necessarily the most talented, the ones in the spotlight, or the traditional leaders. They are:

- Unconventional in their approach.
- Reluctant to take the spotlight.
- Focused on the team's success over their own.

The public often sees the coach or the superstar as the driving force, but the true leader is the captain—the one who quietly shapes the team's destiny.

1. Relentless Focus and Dedication

"They just keep coming."

A surprising truth about human nature is that people often exert more effort when working alone than in a group. This phenomenon is known as social loafing. But there's a remedy: the influence of one individual who embodies total commitment.

The captains of history's most remarkable sports teams demonstrated this. Their dedication wasn't just about natural talent; it was about an unwavering drive to perform at their peak, both in the game and in their preparation.

These leaders didn't just compete; they set the standard for effort. Even when a win seemed certain, they kept the pressure on, pushing their teams to maintain their competitive edge.

Their approach to challenges was unique. Instead of kneeling to pressure, they saw difficulties as puzzles to be solved through perseverance. This mindset transformed obstacles into opportunities for mastery.

Contrary to the belief that natural ability breeds confidence, research suggests otherwise. True self-assurance stems not from innate talent but from how one responds to failure. For these captains, every setback was a step towards greater resilience.

2. Aggressive Play That Tests the Limit of the Rules

"Intelligent fouls."

Sam Walker observed a fascinating trait among the captains of Tier One teams: they often pushed the boundaries of the rules, especially in high-pressure situations. What he found was that these actions were not always impulsive acts performed in the heat of battle. In some cases, these were intentional strategies.

This concept aligns with insights from the 2007 book *Aggression and Adaptation: The Bright Side to Bad Behavior*. A group of American psychologists noted that many of the most ambitious and successful individuals in business exhibit aggressive behaviors. They argue that such behavior can be a pathway to personal growth, goal achievement, and peer respect.

These captains didn't bend rules to cause harm. Their goal was to win. The art lies in balancing aggression with self-control, knowing when to push limits and when to hold back.

These leaders weren't saints. To clinch victory, especially in crucial moments, they sometimes resorted to controversial tactics. The distinguishing factor between a captain who strictly adheres to sportsmanship and one who tests its boundaries lies in their focus. The latter is more driven by the pursuit of victory than by public perception.

3. A Willingness to do Thankless Jobs in the Shadows

"The invisible art of leading from the back."

A common trait among the captains of Tier One teams was their indifference to fame. Their pursuit of the captaincy wasn't for prestige or public recognition; their sole focus was on their team's success. This aligns with a management paradox: those who most eagerly seek leadership roles are often least suited for them, driven more by the allure of status than by commitment to the team's objectives.

These captains were not the typical stars and didn't seek the spotlight. Instead, they embraced practical, supportive roles, often going unnoticed. Whether carrying water or doing other mundane tasks, they chose to position themselves as equals, not superiors. This approach wasn't about diminishing their role but about gaining moral authority and respect, crucial for rallying the team in challenging times.

Their leadership was subtle yet powerful. By serving the team and focusing on the collective need, they created a dynamic where their support was essential, quietly steering the team from the background.

In essence, the most effective way to lead turned out to be through selfless service.

4. A Low-Key, Practical, and Democratic Communication Style

"Practical communication."

Walker's research revealed that Tier One teams thrived in environments where open and frequent communication was the norm. These teams developed a culture where airing grievances, discussing strategies, and offering criticisms happened naturally and swiftly, with everyone encouraged to contribute.

Contrary to popular belief, motivational leadership isn't about grand speeches or perfect timing. The captains of these elite teams often defied this expectation. They weren't known for eloquent speeches; some were even seen as poor communicators, quiet, or inarticulate in traditional terms.

A crucial finding about high-performing teams is the democratic nature of their communication. It's not just about talking; it's about how everyone talks and listens. These leaders engaged with every team member, bringing energy and enthusiasm to their interactions. In Tier One teams, this kind of vibrant, inclusive communication culture was often cultivated and maintained by the captain.

The essence of effective team communication lies not in grand gestures but in a steady flow of practical, down-to-earth, and consistent interactions. It's the everyday exchanges that build the foundation of a cohesive and successful team.

5. Motivates Others With Passionate Nonverbal Displays

"Calculated acts."

The greatest misconception about communication is that it's all about words. However, recent scientific studies have validated what many intuitively understood: our brains are wired to form deep, emotional, and rapid connections with others, often beyond the realm of spoken language. This process of emotional synchronization occurs naturally, whether we're consciously aware of it or not.

Walker's research into Tier One captains showed a recurring pattern. These leaders often resorted to dramatic, unconventional, and sometimes startling actions, especially during critical moments of competition. These instances shared two crucial characteristics:

They did not involve words.

They were intentional.

Despite their lack of formal education in the science of emotional contagion, these captains intuitively recognized times when words fell short. Their actions, without speech, were calculated to evoke strong emotional responses, effectively rallying and motivating their teams in ways that words alone could not achieve.

6. Strong Convictions and the Courage to Stand Apart

"Uncomfortable truths."

As much as we might be conditioned to fear it, conflict inside a team can be a powerful force for good. The greatest captains understood the value of standing apart when necessary, braving what researchers call the "pain of independence."

Research on team conflict has yielded mixed opinions: some view it as hurtful, others as beneficial, and some see it as a complex mix. Key to understanding this is differentiating the types of conflict.

"Personal" conflict stems from dislike or hostility, while "task" conflict arises from disagreements over the team's methods or strategies.

In high-stakes, competitive environments, personal conflict is undoubtedly harmful. However, the elite captains didn't engage in such conflicts. When they caused a stir, it was either to protect their teammates from unfair management decisions or to address practical shortcomings in the team's execution.

Their confrontations weren't about personal grievances; they were strategic, focused on the collective good, and driven by a strong sense of what was right for the team.

7. Ironclad Emotional Control

"Regulating emotion."

There's no doubt that great leaders use emotion to drive their teams. But emotions are multifaceted and can be both empowering and debilitating. Recognizing and managing these emotional dimensions is crucial.

The captains of Tier One teams encountered various challenges that could have easily overwhelmed them with negative emotions, such as injuries, personal tragedies, or political injustices. Not only did they continue to perform during these difficult times, but they also thrived. They demonstrated an extraordinary ability to compartmentalize and control disruptive emotions, prioritizing the team's needs over personal struggles.

While our capacity to regulate emotions is partly influenced by our genetic makeup, there is still room for growth and adaptation. Scientific research suggests that with persistence and practice, we can reshape our emotional responses. The Tier One captains demonstrated this possibility. They displayed, and in some cases, cultivated a remarkable ability to deactivate negative emotions, focusing instead on what was best for the team.

This skill of emotional regulation, often developed over time, was key to their leadership and their teams' success.

Every project, like every sports team, needs a captain. They might not have the title, but they play the role. In my experience managing over $450+ million in construction projects, the success of a project rests on a leader who puts the team's objectives above their own. **Be that captain.**

One of the best ways you can be the captain that your crew needs to succeed is to grow in emotional intelligence.

Tool #3 Emotional Intelligence

Emotional intelligence is the ability to recognize your emotions, understand what they're telling you, and realize how your emotions affect other people.

There are five elements that define Emotional Intelligence: (1) Self-Awareness, (2) Self-Regulation, (3) Motivation, (4) Empathy, and (5) Social Skills.

While IQ is important, EQ is often the determining factor in leadership and executive roles. Developing and using your emotional intelligence is a great way to show others the leader inside of you.

The Heart of Leadership

"To handle yourself, use your head; to handle others, use your heart." - *Eleanor Roosevelt*

We all have two minds. One that thinks and one that feels.

While IQ is important, EQ is often the determining factor in leadership and executive roles.

The ability to recognize, understand, manage, and effectively use emotions—is more critical to workplace success than conventional intelligence or technical skills.

Emotions are important because they guide and motivate us to act. However, they also cause us to act irrationally.

The true value of emotional intelligence lies in its ability to balance these emotional forces.

It equips us with the soft skills needed to perceive, interpret, and manage both our own emotions and those of others.

For roles like project managers, it's not just an added benefit—it's essential. It binds teams, ensures smooth project execution, and creates positive client relationships.

So, let's dive deeper: what exactly is emotional intelligence, and what can you do to improve yours?

Misconceptions About Emotional Intelligence

You should know there are plenty of misconceptions around emotional intelligence.

Before we get into what EI is, let's talk about what it is NOT:

1. Emotional intelligence is not merely "being nice." At times, emotional intelligence can mean getting angry or confronting someone.
2. Emotional intelligence is not about "giving free rein to feelings," but it's about managing feelings to express them effectively and appropriately.

3. Emotional intelligence is not genetically fixed and, unlike IQ, it seems to be largely learned, and in continuous development as we grow.

IQ doesn't predict career success, EI Does.

Emotional intelligence is the ability to recognize your emotions, understand what they're telling you, and realize how your emotions affect other people.

The 5 Main Elements of Emotional Intelligence

In his bestselling book, *Emotional Intelligence: Why it Can Matter More Than IQ*, Goleman identifies the five main elements of "EQ."

While Daniel Goleman was not the first to define emotional intelligence, his writings popularized it and brought EI to a broader audience.

1. Self-Awareness

"He who knows others is wise; he who knows himself is enlightened." - Lao Tzu

People with high emotional intelligence are usually very self-aware. This means being aware of your emotions when they happen, particularly the negative ones like anxiety, depression, and anger. It involves noticing what happens to your body physically and what goes on in your head mentally.

People with high emotional self-awareness can easily reflect on their:

- Mood
- Strengths
- Weaknesses
- Wants

2. Self-Regulation

We usually can't control our emotions when they first surface. However, once we're aware of them, we can manage our response by using techniques to manage negative emotions so that they don't last so long.

Techniques include re-framing a situation that made you angry, increasing physical arousal if depressed, and reducing physical arousal if anxious.

The goal of self-regulation is to take emotional responses and recognize them, but not let them hijack your behavior or control how you handle relationships.

3. Motivation

This is about managing your impulses so they support your goals, not block them.

This means being hopeful and optimistic in the face of difficulty, and using goal-directed self-imposed delayed gratification to achieve goals, and using flow state to reach peak performance.

Motivated people are driven to achieve goals and exceed the expectations set for them.

4. Empathy

Being aware of other people's emotions requires us to have empathy. We must recognize others' feelings and be attuned to their needs and wants.

To have empathy, we need to be calm enough such that we can mirror the other person's physiological state, allowing us to literally feel what they feel.

Empathetic individuals think beyond themselves and remove personal bias to make decisions for a team or organization.

5. Social skills

Unless you live on a deserted island, it will be difficult for you to live a happy life just by managing your mind.

The people around you play a big part in your existence, and only by managing your social interactions with them can you hope to be fulfilled at work and in life.

As you've probably determined, emotional intelligence can be a key to success in your life—especially in your career.

The ability to manage people and relationships is very important in all leaders, so developing and using your emotional intelligence can be a good way to show others the leader inside of you.

Strategies for Improving Your Emotional Intelligence

Emotional intelligence can make you more fulfilled, now one might ask if it's possible to increase it.

The good news is that emotional intelligence **can** be learned and developed. Along with improving your skills in the five areas above, consider these additional strategies:

1. Understanding Your Emotions

Start by focusing on the first pillar, and learn to be aware of and understand your emotions.

If you want to boost your self-awareness and self-management, you can practice using inner dialogues. It will help you identify and name your feelings.

You should ask yourself things like:

- Why am I upset?
- Why am I feeling this way?

- What emotions do I currently feel about my work or my colleagues?
- How do these emotions affect the people around me?
- Am I letting negative emotions affect the way I interact with colleagues or perform my work?

Once you begin naming and tracking emotions, you can assess your weaknesses—times when you let negative feelings (anger, frustration, apprehension, fear, overwhelmed, jealousy, inadequacy, etc.) cloud your judgment and stop you from performing to your best.

2. Giving Feedback: The Artful Criticism

In life, there will be times where we need to tell others to improve, and if we do it wrong, they will get offended and upset at us. But if we do it right, they will be appreciative, and the relationship will improve.

The XYZ Method of *"When you did X, I felt Y, and I'd rather you do Z instead,"* is great because it's focused on how I feel, not on attacking the other person. It also offers a specific solution.

From personal experience, I would also add the following rules about giving an artful critique:

1. **Timing**: They are not busy; their mood is good
2. **Environment**: No one else is present; the environment is comfortable
3. **Intention**: Be considerate, not critical or judging
4. **Tone of Voice**: warm and comfortable
5. **Person**: Make sure you have their trust. Whatever behavior you're advising on, make sure you first set a good example with your behavior.

Giving criticism is difficult for both the giver and the receiver. But if we can do it right, it's highly worth it.

3. Team Performance

In team performance, harmony is the single greatest determinant.

Harmony allows every member to contribute their fullest to the team. If there's any emotional friction, then people cannot offer their best.

Pay close attention to where everyone's hearts are at and put an emphasis on harmony to reduce stress and arguments in your interactions with others.

4. Respond Don't React

If you get very angry during an argument, try to pause to calm down. Strong emotions often stifle your thinking so you can say or do things you'll regret later.

Emotionally intelligent people are intentional about how they **respond** to events.

Remember this simple framework:

E + R = O

Events + **R**esponse = **O**utcome

Outcomes are produced by how you choose to respond, not just by the events we experience. We cannot control Events, but we can control how we respond.

Explore your belief system, and implement this new mindset into your life:

- I do not control my events.
- My response is my choice.
- My behavior produces outcomes.
- The Outcomes I get are not the result of what I want, they are the result of what I choose to do.

The most important decision you make is how you will manage your **responses.**

5. Boosting Empathy

Empathy is putting yourself in another person's shoes to understand their experience without actually going through it yourself.

If you want to improve your empathy, practice seeing the other person's perspective. For example:

- When discussing timelines with trade partners, think about their challenges, remembering the balancing act they perform with multiple projects.
- If you're reviewing blueprints, think about the architect's vision that birthed them.
- If you're calling customer service, think about how it might feel to be on the other end of the conversation.
- If you're going to someone's house, think about how it might feel to be the host.

The more clearly you understand the viewpoint of your trade partner, designer, client, coworker, or friend, the better positioned you are to lead.

6. Boosting Self-Motivation

Adopt a growth mindset. This means seeing failures as learning moments, not just bad luck.

People with this mindset believe they can improve and change. They push forward, even when things get tough. In contrast, those who think they can't change often give up too soon.

To stay motivated, believe in your ability to grow and avoid thinking you're stuck as you are.

7. Reframing

Reframing is a self-regulating technique that involves looking at a situation or problem from a different perspective, like changing the frame of a picture.

It's about finding a more positive or constructive way to view a challenge, which helps in handling emotions better.

Practice it and you will improve your emotional intelligence because you learn to see things in a new light, making you more empathetic and adaptable.

For example:

Imagine you're leading a team, and one member keeps pushing back on your ideas. Instead of thinking, "They're always against me," reframe it to, "They're passionate about the project and want the best outcome." This shift in thinking can make you more patient and open to collaboration.

8. Active Listening

Listening and paying attention to nonverbal cues is vital to developing emotional intelligence.

The way to improve your listening skills is to practice "active listening." This is where you make a conscious effort to hear not only the words that another person is saying but, more importantly, the complete message being communicated.

Active listening helps prevent misunderstandings, shows the proper respect to the person speaking, and gives you the best chance of responding appropriately. It is also an excellent starting point for people to improve their communication skills.

Leaders need Emotional Intelligence not only to manage complex projects effectively but also to lead a fulfilling life and career.

In summary, emotionally intelligent people:

1. Are able to understand their strengths and weaknesses and know where to improve.
2. Have a steady grasp on their emotions and don't act impulsively.
3. Are motivated and productive regardless of circumstances.
4. Are able to put themselves in the shoes of others.
5. Are good team players and capable of letting others shine.

The more that you, as a leader, excel in each of Goleman's five key elements of Emotional Intelligence—self-awareness, self-regulation, motivation, empathy, and social skills—the more effective as a leader you will be.

Vision and EI are absolutely essential for project management. Now that we've tackled that tool, let's check out our final set of tools for being an effective leader.

Tool #4 6 Proven Ways to Increase Your Influence

Leadership is not determined by having a title. It doesn't matter if you are CEO, Director, Superintendent, Project Manager, or Principal; titles do not make leaders—followers do.

Remember that the essence of influence is that people willingly follow your lead. They listen to your advice and seek your wisdom, not out of obligation, but because they value your guidance.

While you might occasionally need to employ tactics like incentives, consequences, or motivational speeches, these should be the exception rather than the rule. The less you rely on these tools, the stronger your influence becomes. Your goal is to tap into people's willpower, navigating through their hesitations and mixed feelings. The strategies outlined below are designed to help you do just that.

#1 Define Your Leadership Style Through Authenticity.

The influence you establish should naturally flow from your unique strengths and character.

Think of a certain archetype of authority and choose one that suits you best.

Consider these familiar archetypes:

- **The Visionary**: Like visionary leaders such as Steve Jobs or Elon Musk, you see what others don't. You challenge the status quo and drive revolutionary changes in technology or thinking.
- **The Reformer**: Think of figures like Martin Luther King Jr. or Nelson Mandela, leaders driven by a deep desire to right wrongs and transform society.
- **The Builder**: These leaders, such as Walt Disney or Sam Walton, create lasting institutions or businesses from the ground up, often pioneering new ways to engage with the world.
- **The Fixer**: Practical and down-to-earth, these leaders are all about solving problems and making things work better, whether they're running a city or a corporation.
- **The Unifier**: Like Mother Teresa or Desmond Tutu, these leaders have a special talent for healing divisions and bringing people together around a common cause.
- **The Coach**: This leader is a true team spirit who thrives when working with others.

There are many more archetypes out there. Recognize which one resonates with you.

Embracing a style that feels natural increases your authenticity and makes your leadership seem almost innate, as though it's woven into your DNA.

The earlier you recognize this style the better; you will have more time to hone it, to adapt to changes, and captivate those around you.

We humans are self-absorbed by nature and spend most of our time focusing inwardly on our emotions, on our wounds, or our dreams.

You want to develop the habit of reversing this as much as possible. You can do this in three ways.

Hone Your Listening Skills

- Absorb yourself in the words and nonverbal cues of others.
- Train yourself to read between the lines of what people are saying.
- Attune yourself to their moods and their needs, and sense what they're missing.
- Do not take people's smiles and nods for reality but rather sense the real emotions that lie beneath.

Earn Respect

- Dedicate yourself to earning people's respect.
- Shift your focus from what you believe others owe you to how you can respect and meet their unique needs.
- Demonstrate your commitment to the group's welfare, not just your own status.

Embrace Responsibility

- Consider being a leader a tremendous responsibility. It is an honor to be in a leadership position. Your team is counting on you to make the right decisions.
- Your primary drive should be to achieve the best outcomes for the group, not getting attention.
- Absorb yourself in the work, not your ego. Feel a deep connection to the group, recognizing that your destinies are intertwined.

If you exude this attitude, people will feel it, and it will open them up to your influence.

They will be drawn to you by the simple fact that it is rare to encounter a person so sensitive to people's moods and dedicated to achieving results.

Develop Your "Third Eye."

Most people are locked in the moment.

They are prone to overreacting and panicking, to seeing only a narrow part of the reality facing the group. They struggle to see alternative ideas or prioritize.

Leaders who stay calm and think beyond the immediate situation can tap into their ability to foresee future trends and unseen opportunities. This skill is referred to as having a "third eye."

These leaders stand out from the group, truly embodying what it means to lead. Here's how you can develop this skill:

1. **Practice Detachment:** Learn to separate yourself from the group's immediate emotions. This detachment allows you to view situations more objectively, free from the influence of intense, momentary reactions.

2. **Elevate Your Perspective**: Regularly force yourself to step back and consider the bigger picture. This broader view helps you see beyond partisan opinions and consider multiple perspectives, including those of outsiders or even adversaries.
3. **Explore Alternatives**: Open your mind to various possibilities and scenarios, particularly those that might unfold adversely. This will enhance your ability to anticipate potential challenges and opportunities.
4. **Plan Strategically**: Once you have a clear vision of the potential path, work backwards to the present. Develop a flexible and thoughtful plan that bridges the gap between today and your future. The thoroughness of your planning will not only boost your confidence but will also inspire confidence in others.

This ability to think ahead and strategize effectively will make your leadership both effective and respected.

#4 Lead by Example.

To encourage discipline in others, you must first be disciplined yourself. To lead others, you must first lead yourself.

As the leader, you must be seen working as hard as or even harder than everyone else.

You set the highest standards for yourself. If there are sacrifices that need to be made, you are the first to make them for the good of the group.

This sets the proper tone. Your team will naturally strive to meet your standards and earn your approval. They will adopt your values and model your behavior without the need for force or constant reminders. This desire to live up to your example is far more effective than any directive you could give.

If team members fail to meet the high standards set, there should be firm and clear consequences. People always respect strength in their leaders, as long as it does not stir up fears of the abuse of power.

If being tough doesn't come naturally to you, develop it, or you will not last very long in the position. You will always have plenty of time to reveal that softer, kinder side that is really you, but if you start soft, you may signal that you are a pushover.

#5 Stir Conflicting Emotions.

Most people are too predictable.

To mix well in social situations, they assume a persona that is consistent—cheerful, pleasing, bold, sensitive. They try to hide other qualities that they are afraid to show.

Be Mysterious

As the leader, you want to be more mysterious to increase your influence. By showing qualities that are slightly contrary, you cause people to pause in their instant categorizations and to think about who you really are. The more they think about you, the larger and more influential your presence.

For example, if you're known for your kindness, occasionally demonstrate firmness to prevent being taken for granted. This complex persona was a key aspect of Martin Luther King Jr.'s compelling leadership.

Balance Your Presence

You must learn to balance presence and absence. Being too accessible can make you appear ordinary, but being too distant can make you unrelatable. Strive for a balance that keeps your presence valued and impactful. Make your appearances count.

Limit Your Speech

Excessive talking can signify insecurity, while selective silence can project strength and control. When you do speak, your words will carry more weight.

Additionally, if you make a mistake, do not over explain or over apologize. Make it clear you accept responsibility and are accountable for any failures, and then you move on.

Avoid appearing defensive and whiny if attacked. You are above that.

#6 Never Appear to Take, Always to Give.

Leaders must avoid the perception that they are taking something people believe is rightfully theirs—be it money, rights, privileges, or personal time.

These actions can create insecurity and damage your credibility, causing people to doubt your intentions and question your leadership. They might wonder, "What more will he take? Is he abusing his power? Has he been fooling us all along?"

- If sacrifices are necessary, lead by example and make sure they're meaningful, not just symbolic.
- Frame any necessary losses as temporary, and clearly communicate how and when these will be restored.
- Position yourself to consistently offer more than you take, which builds trust and loyalty.

Related to this, avoid over-promising. While it might be tempting to make grand promises in the moment, people remember these commitments vividly. Failing to fulfill them not only hurts your credibility but also feels like a breach of trust to your team. Make sure you can deliver on your commitments to maintain your influence and preserve the goodwill you've established.

Leadership styles may change with the times, but one constant remains: the complex relationship between people and authority.

People always have mixed feelings about those in power.

- They want to be led but also want to be free.
- They want to be protected and enjoy success without making sacrifices.
- They both admire a leader one moment and resent them the next.

As a leader, you're always on uncertain ground. This is simply human nature. If you want to lead, you must master these dynamics as soon as possible.

As part of this process, reflect on the impact you have on your team:

- Are you often arguing and facing resistance to your ideas and projects?
- Do people nod as they listen to your advice and then do the opposite?

For those new to leadership, these challenges are common. Initially, ideas from those lower in the hierarchy are often undervalued; the same ideas from a boss might be received differently.

But sometimes it could stem from your own actions. If you're finding resistance, it might be a sign that you're breaking some of the principles described above.

Chapter Takeaways

Here are the main takeaways for our chapter on becoming an effective leader.

- Being a leader is one of the most essential archetypes of project management. If you fail to practice this archetype well, your work life will be chaotic and unproductive.
- **Create a culture of extreme ownership** by taking responsibility for everything on your project.
- **Be the captain your team needs** by having extreme focus, aggressive play, a here-to-serve posture, a practical communication style, passionate nonverbal displays, strong convictions, and iron-clad emotional control.
- **Develop your emotional intelligence** by building self-awareness and self-regulation, motivation, empathy, and social skills.
- **Increase your influence** by defining your leadership style through authenticity, honing your listening skills, earning respect, embracing responsibility, developing your third eye, leading by example, stirring conflicting emotions, and giving, not taking.

By becoming an effective leader, project managers are able to inspire their teams to do their best.

CHAPTER SIX

The Attorney

"Risk comes from not knowing what you are doing."

~ Warren Buffett

When I was working on a multi-million-dollar Nursery & NICU project, I made a big mistake. I skipped truly understanding the project. I thought just glancing at the drawings and specs was enough. I figured I could wing it, and everything would work out. It didn't.

My lack of understanding led to missed details, confused teams, and lack of compensation. We hit snags that could have been avoided if I had taken the time to dig deeper. You see, the contract isn't a weapon, it's the playbook for how we're supposed to act and behave on a project. I didn't take the time to understand it.

I remember the moment it all came crashing down. We were in the middle of a critical phase, and things started to go wrong—really wrong. I felt overwhelmed and out of my depth. I realized then that I had to change my approach.

That experience stayed with me. It changed how I approached every project after that. I learned that being a good project manager isn't just about glancing at drawings or specs. It's about understanding every aspect of the project, including the contract, the general conditions, legal requirements, insurance requirements, and the owner's conditions of satisfaction. I couldn't just wing it anymore.

This story matters because it shows the importance of truly understanding the foundation of your project—the contract. You must know how to navigate the contract, read it, communicate it, and abide by it. Skipping the details might seem like a shortcut, but it leads to bigger problems down the road. If I could summarize this story in one sentence, it would be: Master the details, and you'll master the project.

Why a Project Manager Needs to Be a Great Attorney

In the world of construction project management, everyone is bound by one thing: a contract. As the project manager, you need to know every detail of the project, including the contracts. This knowledge helps you understand your responsibilities, your client's obligations, and any potential liabilities.

If you ignore your role as The Attorney, you leave your team exposed to risks. Understanding contracts is about more than just avoiding lawsuits; it's about managing risk and ensuring the project's success. In both project management and law, it all comes down to managing risk, maintaining good communication, and making sound decisions. These are people skills at their core—skills that protect your team and keep your project on track.

In this chapter, we'll discuss the characteristics of the attorney, and several tools to help you develop those skills effectively: owner contract types and applications, understanding the project, the risk and opportunity manager, and realizing that the biggest risk on a project is you and your own biases.

Characteristics of a Great Attorney

As a project manager who knows how to live into the attorney archetype, you should be able to:

- **Understand the Contract Inside and Out**: Know the terms, obligations, and risks tied to your project.
- **Identify and Manage Risks**: Anticipate potential legal pitfalls and address them before they become issues.
- **Communicate Clearly and Effectively**: Ensure everyone involved understands their roles, responsibilities, and the contract's terms.
- **Negotiate with Confidence**: Stand your ground in contract discussions and protect your team's interests.

Implementing these skills into your work life will help you manage your and your team's liability when it comes to project management.

Owner Contract Types and Application

Your relationship with the client and everyone working under you is defined by the "prime contract." You'll typically encounter the following contract types:

- Construction Management - Preconstruction Agreement (PreCon)
- Construction Management Agreement with a Guaranteed Maximum Price (GMP)
- Construction Management Agreement - Cost Plus a Fee (Cost-Plus)
- Stipulated/Lump Sum Agreement (LS)
- Construction Management Agent for Owner Agreement (Agency)
- Design-Build Agreement (D-B)
- Engineering Procurement Construction Management (EPCM)
- Integrated Project Delivery (IPD)

Because contracts can make or break a project, it's important to develop a contract strategy for successful project management.

Most business projects have many moving pieces and parts and often involve contracting with third parties for supplies and additional services. The contracts you negotiate and sign with these third parties detail how much you pay for those goods and services, when deliverables are due, and who is responsible for various functions.

By embodying The Attorney, you'll protect your team, mitigate risks, and drive your project to successful completion.

Tool #1 Don't Skip Understanding the Project.

When I first started, I thought a quick glance at the drawings and specs would do the trick. Big mistake. It led to missed details, confused teams, delays, and major risks. Now, I make it a priority to thoroughly review every critical document:

- Contract Drawings
- Prime Agreement
- Division 01 Specifications
- Owner's Conditions of Satisfaction
- Schedule

I distill each of these down to key points and ensure the team understands them—clear enough that even a third grader could grasp it.

Managing risk effectively requires a deep understanding of your contract and legal obligations. Construction contracts are packed with complex terms and requirements, so being familiar with the key sections is essential for any project manager.

Here's what you need to know:

Delivery Type

- **Delivery Method**: Know how the project will be delivered.

Contract Essentials

- **Contract Type, Amount, and Fee**: Understand the basic terms.
- **General Conditions**: These are the rules that guide the project.
- **Shared Savings and Change Orders**: How savings are handled and changes are managed.
- **Retention, Billing, and Lien Waiver Requirements**: Ensure compliance to avoid payment delays.
- **Special State Requirements**: Be aware of any regional legal obligations.
- **Liquidated Damages**: Penalties for not meeting the schedule.
- **Insurance**: General liability, builder's risk, and other required coverages.
- **Dispute Resolution and Contingency Breakdown**: How disputes are settled and contingencies are managed.

Other Critical Items

- **Claims Duration**: Timeframe for filing claims.
- **Schedule Delays**: Understand the consequences of falling behind.

- **Change Order Timeliness**: The importance of timely communication and documentation.
- **Payment Terms**: When and how you get paid.
- **Cost Accounting and Audit Rights**: How finances are tracked and audited.
- **Tax Rates**: Ensure compliance with tax obligations.
- **Owner's Representative**: Know who you're dealing with on the owner's side.

Profitability

- **Profit Strategy**: How will the project make money?
- **Financial Pitfalls**: Identify and mitigate potential financial risks.

Key Contract Sections

- **Scope of Work**: A clear, detailed list of tasks for the subcontractor. It sets the legal and financial benchmarks. Make it measurable to avoid future disputes.
- **Schedule**: Start and finish dates for each contractor, subcontractor, or vendor. Understanding this helps you manage the overall project timeline.
- **Change Orders**: The process for altering the contract. Pay close attention to required documents, communication channels, and timing.
- **Payment Terms**: How to invoice and when payments are due. Understand what's required to ensure timely payment.
- **Dispute Resolution**: Steps for resolving disagreements. Know the process to keep things on track.
- **Delays**: Conditions related to excusable and compensable delays. Understand what's covered and what's not.

- **Insurance and Indemnity**: Required coverages and liability protections. Ensure you're fully covered.
- **Termination Clause**: Conditions under which the contract can be ended. Know when and how the contract can be terminated.
- **Communication Protocols**: Specifies the primary contacts and communication methods. Clear lines of communication prevent misunderstandings.
- **Warranty**: The promise of quality from contractors, subcontractors, or vendors.

One of the best ways to manage the risks that you're contracted for is creating a risk and opportunity register. Now that we've covered the details of reading a contract, let's get into the nuts and bolts of managing risk on the job.

Tool #2 The Risk & Opportunity Register

As we've discussed at length in this book, the vast majority of construction projects are delivered late—and, unfortunately—over-budget. Solving this problem is one of the primary goals of "the Attorney." We can deploy a number of methods and tools for achieving more valuable projects completed more efficiently, including the risk & opportunity register.

The nature of traditional project delivery methods such as Design-Bid-Build can be chaotic and disorganized, with a lack of clear communication leading to re-work, waste, and new, unexpected costs piling on top of one another to cover up for mistakes and poor planning.

One of the principal goals of Lean is to eliminate waste by improving the flow of communication and increase transparency between project teams. This is one of the main functions of the risk & opportunity register.

A risk & opportunity register is one of the most effective Lean tools for anticipating and managing risk, allowing teams to communicate in order to make crucial risk-mitigating decisions before waste accrues and the project becomes over-budget. The tool also allows the team to identify potential opportunities to add value or improve the schedule of the project.

What is a Risk & Opportunity Register?

A Risk & Opportunity Register is part of the overall strategy of building a visual workspace. It allows risks and opportunities to be identified and assessed early, and allows the team to apply intellectual capital rather than financial capital to mitigate or avoid risks, and to monitor and take advantage of opportunities

Risk & opportunity registers are beneficial for all types of construction projects. However, they are found most frequently in projects using Integrated Project Delivery. In those projects, a risk & opportunity register is mandatory since every member of the project team has a stake in the financial success of the project.

The risk & opportunity register itself is a shared document that allows team members to discuss risks & opportunities together, then pool their knowledge together, thus promoting a mindset of Respect for People. Having a record of previous risks and the ways in which they were addressed also allows the team to revisit and revise current strategies, leading to Continuous Improvement.

As the name suggests, the risk & opportunity register has two separate sides, the risks and the opportunities.

How to Utilize a Risk & Opportunity Register

The following are some tips for making the most of your risk & opportunity register.

Be Thorough

When discussing the register with your team, try to determine all possible risks and opportunities that could impact the project throughout all stages of the project's completion.

What are some things that could go wrong? In the spirit of Continuous Improvement, refer back to problems that have arisen in previous projects you've been involved with. Could a similar problem arise in this new project?

With regards to opportunities, are there possible improvements you've always wanted to try in a project that you might get the chance to now? Plan for those early to ensure they aren't forgotten.

Plan Early

Ensure that the register is a key part of the project planning process from the beginning. The sooner potential risks are identified, the easier it will be for the team members to anticipate solutions to those problems so they don't cause a panic when they turn into a reality.

Revisit Often

It has taken me many years to realize that identifying risks at the beginning is not enough. Don't pay attention to just the initial risks.

To maintain an effective grasp of reality, one must undergo a continuous cycle of interaction with the environment to assess constant changes.

Looking back, I'd monitor and update your risk and opportunity register **every week** using the OODA cycle:

- **Observe:** Collect the latest data.
- **Orient:** Analyze what the data means.
- **Decide:** Choose the best course of action.
- **Act:** Take swift action and repeat this cycle weekly.

This way you can make sure your biggest issues are covered with the right people at the right time.

The team should put together a process for updating and consulting the register so that it remains a standard piece of the workflow. Effectively communicate to the team who is responsible for updating the list, deciding what items should be discussed at the upcoming meeting, and allocating resources to determine potential solutions to future problems.

Collaborate

Encourage involvement from the entire team to discuss risks and opportunities.

Furthermore, the team should always come into meetings with a mindset of problem solving, exhausting every possible avenue before settling on a binary "yes" or "no" answer to an unexpected change in schedule or circumstance in the project.

Know Your Priorities

Tackle the highest priority and highest risk probability concerns first, and discuss lower priority risks afterwards.

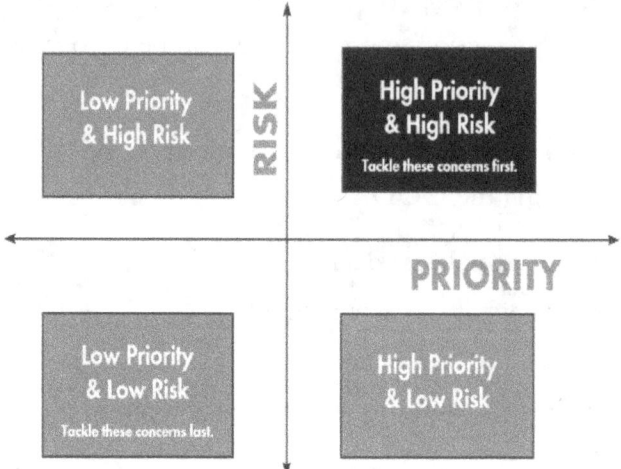

The register itself is a list of line items that include potential risks and opportunities, including the likelihood of the event in question coming to pass and the financial hit that would come with it.

The biggest risk that you need to manage may surprise you. When you're considering risk and risk management, it's important to realize that the biggest risk is you.

Tool #3 The Biggest Risk Is You

It's tempting to think that projects fail because the world throws surprises at us:

- Price and scope changes
- Accidents
- Weather
- New management
- The list goes on…

But this is shallow thinking.

Consider the Sydney Opera House. It didn't fail because Jørn Utzon couldn't predict every single challenge; it failed because he took the inside view on his project and didn't study how failure typically occurs for large-scale architectural projects.

Why didn't he?

Because focusing on the particular case and ignoring the class is what human psychology inclines us to do.

The greatest threat Utzon faced wasn't out in the world; it was in his own head, in his **behavioral biases.**

This is true for every one of us and every project. Which is why your biggest risk is YOU.

This tool features an academic paper by Prof. Bent Flyvbjerg covering the top 10 most important behavioral biases in project planning and management. It is one of the most read articles in the Project Management Journal.

Each bias is defined, and its impacts on project management are explained, with examples.

They are the biases most likely to trip up planners and managers and negatively impact project outcomes, if the biases are not identified and dealt with up front and during delivery.

According to the research findings, the top 10 behavioral biases are:

1. Strategic Misrepresentation

The tendency to intentionally and systematically distort or misstate information for strategic purposes. Also known as political bias, strategic bias, or power bias.

Ever seen a project or an idea made to look better than it is? That's strategic misrepresentation. People are naturally inclined to twist facts and sugarcoat things to get funding or approval. Like when a contractor underestimates costs to win a bid, only to face budget overruns later. Recognize this and always triple-check your assumptions.

2. Optimism Bias

The tendency to be overly optimistic about the outcome of planned actions, including overestimation of the frequency and size of positive events and underestimation of the frequency and size of negative ones.

We all love a good success story, but optimism bias makes us think everything will go perfectly. Remember the last time a project timeline seemed too good to be true? That's optimism bias at work. Always watch your downside.

3. Uniqueness Bias

The tendency to see one's project as more singular than it actually is.

It's easy to see our projects as one-of-a-kind. When in reality, it's part of a larger class of comparable projects. That's uniqueness bias. Even the most unique projects have similarities with past ones. Learn from previous projects to avoid repeating mistakes. No need to reinvent the wheel every time.

4. The Planning Fallacy

The tendency to underestimate costs, schedule, and risk and overestimate benefits and opportunities. Just as the name suggests, the planning fallacy can lead to poor planning, causing us to make decisions that ignore the realistic demands of a task (be it time, money, energy, or something else).

It also leads us to downplay the elements of risk and luck; instead, we focus only on our own abilities—and an overly optimistic assessment of our abilities at that. Always add strategic buffer time and budget to your plans.

5. Overconfidence Bias

Overconfidence bias is the tendency to have excessive confidence in one's own answers to questions and to not fully recognize the uncertainty of the world and one's ignorance of it.

Are you overly sure about your predictions? Overconfidence bias can blind you to uncertainties. It's like betting everything on one plan without a backup. Always question your assumptions and consider multiple outcomes.

6. Hindsight Bias

The tendency to see past events as being predictable at the time those events happened. Also known as the I-knew-it-all-along effect.

Thought you "knew it all along" after a project fails? Hindsight bias makes us believe past events were predictable. Instead, focus on learning from mistakes without assuming you could have seen them coming.

7. The Availability Bias

The tendency to think that events which are easier to remember are more likely to happen.

Remembering only the most recent or dramatic events? That's availability bias. It skews our perception of what's likely. If a recent project had a major issue, you might overestimate its frequency. Balance recent experiences with historical data.

8. The Base Rate Fallacy

The tendency to ignore general statistics and instead focus on specific stories. If you play poker and assume different odds than those that apply, you are subject to the base rate fallacy and likely to lose. The objective odds are the base rate.

Stay away from thinking your project will be the exception to the rule. Always consider the broader data. If most projects in your field face certain risks, so will yours.

9. Anchoring

The tendency to rely too heavily, or "anchor," on one trait or piece of information when making decisions, typically the first piece of information acquired on the relevant subject.

Anchoring is basing decisions on the first piece of information you get. For example, if the first cost estimate is low, you might stick to it despite new, higher estimates. Always seek several data points before letting your thoughts take control.

10. Escalation of Commitment

The tendency to justify increased investment in a decision, based on the cumulative prior investment, despite new evidence suggesting the decision may be wrong. Also known as the sunk cost fallacy.

This is when you feel urged to stick with a decision because you've invested so much in it. Think of a project or an initiative you knew was failing but kept funding anyway. Cut your losses early to avoid bigger failures down the line.

Conclusion

From my experience in project management, I've seen firsthand how these biases can derail even the best-laid plans. Recognizing and addressing them must be a priority.

For instance, during one of my first projects, I got caught falling into both the planning fallacy and optimism bias. We were working on a new healthcare facility, and I was way off about meeting a tight deadline. I overestimated our resources and underestimated the variability. Midway through the project, we faced unexpected supply chain issues. The delays piled up, and the client was frustrated. Knowing what I know now about these biases, I would have built in more buffer time and managed expectations more realistically.

In closing, I encourage you to become more familiar with the top 10 behavioral biases in project management. You can gain a lot more influence over your project outcomes if you are. It boils down to:

- Structured decision-making processes.
- Iterative feedback loops.
- Leveraging historical data.

If you can bake these systems into your execution and leadership, there is an opportunity to reduce the impacts of these biases, leading to more successful projects.

Chapter Takeaways

Here are the main takeaways for our chapter on becoming an effective attorney.

- Being an Attorney is essential to the success of your project. If you don't know your or your clients' responsibilities, you are setting you and your team up for failures, lawsuits, and other liabilities.

- **Understand the project** before you start by reviewing the delivery type, contract essentials, all critical items, profitability, and key contract sections.

- **Use a risk and opportunity register** by being thorough, planning early, revisiting often, collaborating, and knowing your priorities.

- **Realize that the biggest risk on any given project is YOU.** You may think your plan is foolproof because it's yours. Keep your eyes open and analyze every situation with an understanding of your own biases, so you can make wise choices and protect you and your team from liability.

By becoming an effective attorney, project managers are able to protect themselves and their teams from lawsuits and unnecessary legal fees. Learning how to read contracts well comes with patience and practice. Use this chapter to help you develop these skillsets.

CHAPTER SEVEN

The Accountant

"Accounting is the language of business."

~ Warren Buffett

I remember a Project Manager who had all the right intentions but lacked the financial skills that are critical to running the business side of project management. He was eager to lead and had been promoted quickly, but he didn't have a solid grasp of the financial side of the job. Managing budgets, tracking costs, and forecasting were foreign concepts to him.

Despite his enthusiasm, he struggled to account for progress correctly. He couldn't reconcile the numbers with the actual work being done on-site, which led to constant discrepancies in the reports. When it came time to review the project's financial health, he couldn't explain where the money was going or how it aligned with the project's progress. He relied heavily on others to provide the numbers and often just accepted them at face value without digging deeper.

This lack of financial oversight led to serious issues. The project started bleeding money, and deadlines were missed because the resources weren't being allocated correctly. He didn't understand the importance of cash flow or how to use financial data to influence the project's direction. As a result, he couldn't make informed decisions or adjust the project plan to stay on track.

The situation became untenable when the project started slipping further behind schedule, and costs spiraled out of control. The project executive had to step in to assess what was going wrong.

During a tense meeting, it became clear that the Project Manager couldn't account for the project's financials or provide a clear path to recovery. He admitted that he wasn't equipped to manage the numbers and didn't know how to turn things around.

In the end, the decision was made to reassign him that required less business acumen. He was moved to a position where he wouldn't have to manage budgets or influence project outcomes directly. The project eventually got back on track under new leadership, but the experience served as a stark reminder: without mastering the financial aspect, a Project Manager can't truly steer the project to success.

Why a Project Manager Needs to Be a Great Accountant

Contractors and project managers do three things: get work, do work, and keep score. Which of these topics do you think gets the least recognition and training in the industry? That's right: scorekeeping. You are reading this section to become better at keeping score for the company.

The ability to create a successful financial outcome is a primary job requirement if you want to build a career as a project leader. One of the biggest client expectations that you need to tackle is staying within your client's budget. If you have unreasonable expectations of costs, or you don't manage your budget well, you will likely face disappointed and angry clients, or even lawsuits.

Financial savvy is a critical leadership skill in every industry. Accounting can come off as being a dry topic, but it is essential for any project manager. The goal of this chapter is to improve your business acumen as you continue to run the toughest projects in your market.

In this chapter, we'll discuss how the biggest firms die, and three tools to help you develop these skills: accounting practices for the construction industry, change management, and forecasting.

How the Biggest and the Best Firms Die

In 2007, FMI invested a significant effort in a comprehensive study to determine the causes and effects of contractor failure. The findings are not likely to surprise you. The most frequent causes of contractor failure are:

1. Unrealistic growth – volume obsession.
2. Entry into new markets or types of projects.
3. Poor project selection.
4. Bad contracts and projects.
5. Insufficient capital or profit generation.
6. Poor financial management.
7. Poor leadership.
8. Owner/customer bankruptcy.
9. Economic weakness.
10. Changes in banking or surety relationships.

Poor financial management is reflected in some way in every one of these top ten causes. The bad jobs that many contractors experience account for significant margin erosion and determine deterioration of value creation in the industry. Think about your company—if you could recover all the lost profits from bad jobs over the years, how much would your company's net worth increase?

Let's take a look at the best practices for the construction industry so you can save your company millions of dollars.

Tool #1 Accounting Practices for the Construction Industry

As a project manager, you need a basic understanding of why the body of knowledge that we call "accounting" exists. Picture the construction industry as it would be if we had no building codes or standards of construction. Look at some third-world countries and you may see what sort of problems result. The same is true in financial accounting. Practices, rules, and regulations exist to drive standardization in financial reporting. The infrastructure is called **generally accepted accounting practices (GAAP)**.

Accounting Practices for the Construction Industry

An underlying principle of accounting is the concept of matching. Matching is about pairing up the income and expense in the period when they are incurred to measure economic performance.

1. **Cash Basis Accounting:** Under the cash basis method of accounting, income and expenses are matched in the period when paid or received.
2. **Accrual Method Accounting:** In the accrual method of accounting, income and expenses are matched in the period when incurred or accrued. Using the accrual method of accounting is the only generally accepted (GAAP) method of accounting for long-term construction contracts in the construction industry.
3. **Percentage of Completion Method:** The percentage of completion method of accounting is used for long-term construction contracts. It is a form of accrual accounting, adding the percentage completed as the way to match the right amount of income and expense in the calendar year,

quarter, or month. This is the method of accounting for projects that will last longer than one year.

4. **Completed Contract Method:** Small projects can use the completed contract method of accounting because their projects are not typically considered long-term. In the accounting world, long-term generally means one year or longer. Small projects and home building are examples that use this method of accounting. Under this method, income and expenses associated with each home are recorded in the period the home is sold. Income and expenses are not recognized along the way during construction of the home, even though the period to complete the home is several months and extends beyond the quarter or year end when the company reports its earnings.

5. **Units of Production Method:** Road builders use the units of production method of accounting for significant portions of their work. Estimates are prepared based on quantities for installation and a quoted or stated rate per unit. Engineers and/or project staff physically observe the number of units installed for the period. The billing is based on these "engineered" estimates, and corresponding payments are made on that basis.

The goal of each method is to match the income and expenses in the period in which they are truly earned or incurred. The economic result (the difference between the expenses and income) is the profit or loss from operations during the reporting period.

Variations of these methods can be found in long-term construction contracts and include things like cost-plus contracts, time and materials contracts, and other cost-plus-fee arrangements. As with all methods, the goal is to properly match the income and expenses as they are incurred and/or accrued.

The complexity of construction projects and the accounting methods used to manage them cannot be underestimated. The management skill to handle costs, plus constant changes in the scope of work and building requirements, is a major challenge.

Let's look at some tools to help you manage that change.

Tool #2 Change Management

Just like the seasons inevitably turn, project change is a given. It's not a matter of if it will happen, but when. If you know that, you make a plan on how to deal with change, right?

I didn't on one of my first projects, and it nearly cost me my job… It's a classic story of a young and hungry guy who is trying to impress the boss with one of his first big projects.

Early in my career, I was overseeing a significant healthcare facility project. I was confident, maybe overly so. As the project progressed, change requests began trickling in. In my eagerness to please the client and assert my capability, I accepted and implemented changes without a formal review or tracking system.

It seemed manageable at first. However, as the project neared its end, I faced a startling revelation. Numerous change orders had accumulated, many slipping through the cracks of my informal tracking system. This oversight led to a significant budget overrun and a client who was far from pleased.

Reflecting on this experience, I identified two fundamental issues:

1. **A People Problem:** There was a lack of clarity regarding roles, behavior, and responsibilities in handling changes.
2. **A System Problem:** The absence of effective tools and a defined process for managing change requests was evident.

Despite these challenges, we managed to deliver a successful project. But, this experience underscored the importance of a systematic approach to change management in construction projects.

What is a Change Request?

You've initiated your project, got everything planned out, and head down into execution. And then, something pops up. There are different kinds of change that we'll cover soon. But let's set the definition first:

A change request is a formal proposal to modify the initial project plan, potentially impacting scope, budget, resources, timelines, or quality standards. These adjustments can emerge from various levels, including owners, contractors, or subcontractors, and stem from diverse reasons.

Change requests can arise due to client demands, team insights, unexpected external factors, or the recognition of overlooked requirements.

Completing a change order correctly minimizes risk, improves the chances of approval, and helps contractors get paid faster.

Not All Change is Created Equal

Change is multifaceted, and understanding its different forms is key to effective management.

There are four broad categories of change:

1. **Strategic Change**: This involves significant shifts in project or organizational direction, often necessitating major alterations to your project plan. For instance, a company-wide reorganization could lead to a reevaluation of project objectives or resources.

2. **Anticipated Change**: These are changes you foresee and plan for, overlapping with risk management. An example could be a delay in the launch of a new piece of equipment or technology that you had already factored into your project timeline.
3. **Reactive Change**: Triggered by unforeseen events, reactive changes require you to adapt your plan without complete overhaul. An example might be the sudden departure of a key project member.
4. **Incremental Change**: Often linked with scope creep, this type of change involves gradual, often minor adjustments that collectively can have a significant impact. For instance, continuous small additions or alterations to project scope could lead to major shifts over time.

In any case, change management starts with change identification. Sounds obvious, but change can often infiltrate a project unnoticed.

And that's why you should make a change management plan.

Your Change Management Plan

A change management plan sounds like a pile of paperwork. But trust me, it's not, and it's worth the effort.

It involves thinking through how you'll deal with change when it hits, and can often be re-used for future projects.

A change management plan ensures that you answer the most important questions that you also answered when you planned your project:

- Who
- What
- Why

- When
- Where
- How

Let's walk through each step 1 by 1.

Step 1: Review Roles & Responsibilities

Effective change management starts with clear roles and responsibilities:

1. **Requesting a Change**: Determine who is authorized to propose changes. This could be certain team members or client representatives.
2. **Evaluating Change Requests**: Decide who will assess and review the change requests. Typically, this includes the project manager along with key team members.
3. **Authorizing Changes**: Identify who has the final say in approving changes. Often, this is the client or a designated authority.
4. **Timelines for Communication**: Set specific time frames for notifying relevant parties about a change and for reviewing and submitting change requests.

In most instances, the construction contract dictates the change order process. The contract will provide specific guidelines on how to manage and process the change order.

Treat the contract as your change management playbook, ensuring your change management strategy aligns with its stipulations.

Step 2: Standardize Change Requests

To streamline the change request process:

1. **Utilize a Standard Form**: Implement a standard form for all change requests. This approach helps filter out non-

essential requests and ensures you receive all necessary information for evaluation.
2. **Incorporate Technology**: Consider using change management software. This tool simplifies tracking, approving, and managing project change orders, offering time and cost savings.
3. **Key Form Elements**: Your form should make sure that a requester explains:
    - Who is requesting the change.
    - What the expected impact is of the change.
    - Why this change is being requested.
    - Photos & Visuals when relevant to support the explanation.

By standardizing change requests, you facilitate a more efficient and effective evaluation process, ensuring that only relevant and well-justified changes are considered.

Step 3: Evaluate Incoming Changes

When you get a change, you'll need to assess the impact and make a recommendation whether to accept it or not.

You'll need to review for two critical pieces:

1. **Entitlement:** Determine if the change is justified.
2. **Equability:** Verify if the change is fair, accurate, and reasonable.

In projects, you have four variables:

- Time
- Scope
- Quality
- Budget

A change always has primary impact on one of those variables. But if you touch one, you touch all four. They're all connected. Think through the consequences of accepting the change.

Based on that, advise your client clearly on whether to accept the change, outlining its effects, like a potential delay or cost increase. Frame your advice with specific conditions for implementation to guide the client's decision.

"Business critical, 2-week delay, $1M extra contract value. I suggest we do it, but under the condition of X, Y, and Z."

That's the conversation you want to have with your clients.

Step 4: Submit Vetted Change Orders

The contract may spell out the specific change order form a contractor should use, and how to submit it.

What's most important is that it contains the key pieces of information that can help a property owner or architect approve the change.

Here are six things every change order should include:

1. Project and Contact Information: Identifies the project and relevant contacts.
2. Dates of Change Events: Specifies when the change occurred or will occur.
3. Details of the Work:
    a. The Who: Lists who is affected or involved in the change.
    b. The What: Describes the work involved in the change (Including photos and visuals).
    c. The Why: The actual reason triggering the change and why the change is necessary.
4. Updated Schedule

5. Cost of the Change
6. Updated Contract Value: The original contract value, the cumulative value of past approved change orders, and the cost of the current change order.

Step 5: Build a Change Log

A change log is a document where you track all change requests. You mark them as accepted or rejected, and summarize what the impact of the decision is.

A change log will help you keep track of the overall project, as many small changes add up to big deviations.

Incorporating the right technology into your management plan enhances these benefits. Advanced project leaders use Universal Change Logs, allowing team-wide access to the financial records and ensuring seamless project closeouts.

Step 6: Communicate Your Changes

This sounds obvious, but gets missed often. If you accept changes, tell your team and your stakeholders about it.

Tell them what change you've accepted and what the impact is. Then explain how you'll deal with the change and what parts of the initial plan are adjusted.

Project management is communication. Make the implicit explicit, and manage expectations. And above all: check if you were understood.

Step 7: Implement and Control the Change

Once you've approved and communicated the change, you'll need to make sure it gets done.

Put checks in place when you accept the changes, and mark them as done in your change log when the change is implemented.

Communicate to the stakeholders and the person who requested the change that you're done, and move on with implementation.

I know what you're thinking: this sounds like work.

And you're right. It is work. But in practice:

- 90% is the same for every project you do.
- In smaller projects, most steps involve the same people.
- Authorizing changes by the stakeholders can be batched or even sent as email. Not nearly as formal or cumbersome as it sounds.

Controlling change, risk, and stakeholders are the differentiators between administrative project managers and strategic project leaders.

Build a process, follow it, and turn change from a risk into an opportunity to stand out.

Now that we know how to manage change from risk to an opportunity, let's look at how we can forecast well so we can budget effectively in the workplace.

Tool #3 Forecasting – The Art of Financial Foresight

Years ago, I was walking through my jobsite with one of my company's senior leaders. I'll be honest, I was nervous. This was my first big project as the lead, and I was eager to show off our progress. We had everything under control: the site was safe, we were on schedule, and our work was quality.

My boss nodded along, offering occasional comments that felt like mild breezes against the backdrop of our achievements. But then, just as we were finishing up, he paused, turning to face me with a question that hit me like a ton of bricks.

"How much jingle you got?" he asked, searching for the depth of our financial safety net—the extra money set aside for unexpected problems. His question took me by surprise. I didn't have the numbers, so I fumbled for a response. His disappointment was evident.

"You need to have this information at your fingertips," he told me before walking away. That moment changed everything for me. I promised myself I'd never be unprepared again. I'd always know exactly where we stood financially, down to the last penny.

This experience taught me the importance of **financial forecasting,** one of the most important tools to have under your belt as a project manager.

What is Cost Forecasting?

Forecasting is the process of predicting the total costs and outcomes of a project. It uses data from past projects and the current one to make these predictions.

The goal is to update the original budget with real project progress and any changes that happen along the way. This helps spot any budget issues early and fix them quickly.

Each month, you generate a report looking at: (1) how much money you've spent, (2) how much of the project is done, and (3) estimate what it will cost to finish. You also need to understand your project's productivity. Productivity can be both a leading and lagging indicator of performance.

Productivity = Output / Input

It is useful for understanding how we are doing now and where improvement is needed or possible. Understanding productivity and the results achieved is the first step in estimating costs.

The more up-to-date and accurate your information, like direct costs, fixed prices, work left to complete, and how fast you're getting things done, the better your forecast will be. This level of understanding helps set the foundation of the costs on the project.

Project witness:

- Only track actual productivity sporadically.
- Assume or rely on the superintendent to know what work remains.
- Rely on the field or estimate to determine remaining work costs.
- Think cost to complete is purely science-based and formulaic.
- Can only identify project overruns at 80%+ completion.

Project leaders:

- Understand actual productivity on completed work.
- Accurately estimate remaining work and associated costs.
- Estimate total project cost at completion.
- Recognize that cost estimation is both a science and an art.
- Identify project overruns early, at around 20% completion.

A solid forecast lets your team make smart decisions, plan for the future, avoid unexpected problems, and keep everyone informed about the project's money situation.

How to Create an Accurate Forecast

Creating an accurate forecast doesn't have to be daunting. Here's how to streamline the process.

Before you begin diving into the numbers:

1. **Understand your contract:** Know the ins and outs of your project's agreement.
2. **Review past financials:** Look at your previous financial statements for insights.
3. **Assess Your schedule, issues, and risks:** Get a clear picture of where your project currently stands.

With a solid understanding of these elements, you're ready to craft your forecast.

The Forecasting Formula:

Estimate at Completion ("EAC") is the "Money already spent on the project (AC)" plus the "Money that will be spent to complete the project (ETC)";

EAC = Actual Cost (AC) + Estimate to Complete (ETC)

In the above formula, you can get the actual cost (AC) from your financial or timesheet system. Now, the question is how to calculate the remaining cost, or ETC.

Step 1: Categorize Your Expenses

Every project has a bunch of different types of cost that will be required to bring your project to life.

Break down your costs into categories:

- Labor

- Materials
- Equipment
- Vehicles
- Software
- Misc. other costs

This helps you see where your money is going.

Step 2: List Your Expenses

Now start listing all your expenses and how much they cost per month or per week.

Detail your expenses, including their frequency (monthly or weekly) and cost. Adding them to your change manage ment system or an Excel sheet makes this step manageable.

1. Assign a name to each expense.
2. Determine its nature (fixed amount, time-based, percentage of revenue).
3. Classify it (labor, materials, etc.).
4. Note if it's a constant, variable, or one-time cost.

Example Expenses:

- Project Manager Kyle (labor, hours per month)
- Office Equipment (material, flexible, one-time expense)
- Scaffold Rental (material, fixed, monthly)
- Forklift Rental (equipment, fixed, monthly)

Step 3: Adjust Your Budgets

Your initial budgets might need tweaking as the project progresses.

For each expense, record your:

- Total Budget

- Cost to date
- Estimated cost to complete

Using the formula, these data points will identify your potential savings or overruns, giving you a clear financial snapshot of your project.

Bringing It All Together

I've mentioned it before, but it bears repeating: as a project manager, your role involves turning the unseen into something tangible and manageable.

Creating an accurate forecast is a prime example of this. It allows your team to navigate financial aspects of the project efficiently and accurately, right from the start.

If the above seems like a lot of work, remember two things:

1. **Forecasts evolve with your projects.** Once you've established a solid forecasting process, it becomes a tool that adapts and grows with you, offering long-term benefits that can guide decision-making for years to come.
2. **You'll mostly consult your forecast when necessary.** Each time you do, it's a potential issue or question that you've preemptively addressed. That's leverage right there!

So, what's the first cost you'll predict with your new forecasting tool?

In construction forecasting, historical data and increased visibility are important for making those smart decisions.

The Importance of Cash in the Bank

The only financial sin in business that is not forgivable is running out of cash. If you are out of cash, you are out of business.

Surprisingly, more construction companies fail during economic booms than during recessions. Why? Because growth eats up cash.

For contractors, expansion means spending more money upfront on estimates, proposals, planning, staffing, and site expenses—long before any bills are sent to customers.

Sending a bill doesn't instantly bring in cash. Contractors are still responsible for all costs until the customer pays. That period of investing cash before getting paid is where contractors, especially in a growth mode, get into financial trouble.

Here's how to stay on top of your cash flow:

The Liquidity Indicator

Contractors with strong liquidity have the competitive advantage.

Liquidity is your ability to have enough cash to cover short-term liabilities like loans, payroll, and expenses.

A liquidity indicator is an easy financial calculation that uses the income statement and balance sheet accounts to measure if work-in-process ("WIP") from operations is providing cash or using cash. It involves six accounts:

Current Asset Accounts:

- Accounts Receivables
- Accounts Receivables Retention
- Cost and Earnings in Excess of Billings (Underbillings)

Current Liability Accounts:

- Accounts Payable
- Accounts Payable Retention
- Billings and Earnings in Excess of Costs (Overbillings)

You calculate liquidity by comparing these accounts. **Accounts receivables** are money that will be converted to cash in the future, and underbillings are direct costs that have been incurred but not yet billed for. **Accounts payables** are money the company will have to pay out, and billings in excess of earnings are services the company owes to its customers.

Your goal is to run your project as liquid as possible.

The 3 Views of Liquidity:

1. **Collections vs. Payments:** Net cash pending collection vs. net cash waiting to be paid.
    a. Positive Number: You are funding your own work-in-process.
    b. Negative Number: The project owner is funding the work-in-process.
2. **Average Days Outstanding:** Average days outstanding is the most common way of calculating and displaying the liquidity indicator. This calculation tells you the number of days the cash is held in each account.
    a. Formula: Account balance / (Project's annual revenue / 365 days)
3. **Financial Modeling:** The ability to predict impact of changes before they happen.
    a. For example, reducing collection time from 38.9 days to 30 days can free up additional [$X] amount of cash to invest or capture discounts.

b. Additional Cash Generation = Average Days of Accounts Receivable Improvement x Average Daily Revenue

All three views help frame how cash is being used on projects and its impact on the business.

The Impact of Change Orders

Change orders can be a major challenge to liquidity. They arise from multiple factors and must be billed promptly.

Did you know that unless you bill for the changes, your company will end up paying for all costs and losing any potential profit associated with the change order?

Best-in-class managers are prepared to handle change orders, and so are their clients.

Your job as a project manager is to sell the additional value resulting from the change order. If the customer is convinced of the value, then they should be willing to pay for the additional work in a timely manner.

Tip: Don't let change orders roll over. Get them approved and billed right away to avoid weak bargaining positions at project end. Have a method for handling them in place at the start of the project, and make sure the client is aware of and on board with this process.

The Right Behaviors for Positive Cash Flow

Managing the risk of getting paid is like any other good habit; it is all a matter of creating deliberate practices and having the discipline to apply them.

Here are some simple habits that can be put in place to ensure timely invoicing and collections:

1. **Set calendar reminders:** You don't have to wait until the 25th to engage in the billing process. Start the process on the 20th, and list the key steps to complete on time.
2. **Send standard forms regularly:** Make it easy on your team by sending an email every month with all the forms they need to get the billings turned in accurately. The more you can do to simplify and automate your team's tasks, the greater chance of them complying.
3. **Follow up with reminders:** After the forms have been sent, check in on progress. A quick call or email helps everyone stay on track.
4. **Schedule review time:** Set aside time before the 25th to review draft invoices with your team. Early revisions help catch mistakes.
5. **Preliminary client conversations**: During job meetings, discuss key billing items and any unusual charges. Remind them you are going to submit the invoice by the 25th.
6. **Submit and follow up:** Once you send the invoice, confirm receipt with your contact. Make sure it's moving towards approval. It's also worth double checking that their accounting system is set up to distribute within the days specified in the contract.
7. **Ask for Payment:** If the check is not in your hands by 35 days from the time the invoice is sent, check on it. Be professional and courteous as usual. There is nothing wrong in expecting to be paid as outlined in the contract.

How to Accelerate Your Project's Profitability

I'm going to explain how to accelerate cash in the bank for your construction projects.

Why is this important? Because when an invoice slips to 60 or 90 days outstanding, the lack of cash can quickly erode your project's profitability. Learning to manage this will keep your projects liquid and your business thriving.

The goal is to have the project owner finance their own project, which seems like a reasonable expectation. Unfortunately, many people struggle with this because they don't implement best practices from the start. These techniques shorten the time between cost and incurred and cash received.

But don't worry, I'm here to explain how you can overcome these problems.

Step 1: Customer Due Diligence

Knowing your client's financial health can prevent poor investments and confirm project funding is secure.

Before starting any project, I encourage you to look into the client's creditworthiness and confirm project funding. This step can save you from financial headaches down the line.

Step 2: Negotiate Up Front

Contractors often accept payment terms that are too lenient.

Instead of accepting terms, negotiate aggressive payment terms upfront. Make sure your contract includes a schedule of values that aligns with approved milestones. This keeps billings ahead of project costs, so you're always overbilled rather than under-billed.

Step 3: Set High Goals

Setting high goals helps you strive for excellence and ensures better cash flow management.

Aim to be the best in class for collections. Track your performance against top quartile benchmarks for your construction type. This continuous improvement will keep your projects financially healthy.

Step 4: Train Your Team

A well-trained team can significantly impact your cash flow.

Train project managers and field leaders on best practices. Share with them that satisfied customers pay faster and teach them techniques to consistently provide value throughout the project. This reduces any reasons for payment delays.

Step 5: Bill and Collect

Delayed, inaccurate, or incomplete invoices are the most common cash flow problems.

Make sure your invoices are timely, accurate, and consistent with contract terms. Use pre-approved forms to meet client accounting needs. Know your customer's payment practices in advance and adhere to them strictly.

Step 6: Go Ugly Early

Addressing issues immediately prevents them from becoming bigger problems.

If a problem arises, deal with it early. Assertive collection efforts from the beginning show your client that you're serious about payments.

Step 7: Do Great Work

The bottom line is quality work leads to prompt payments.

A company that performs excellent work, provides great service, and maintains discipline in billing and collecting, is usually paid on time.

If a client is delaying payment for no obvious reason, ask them why, preferably face-to-face.

Step 8: Price Promptly

Quick approval of change orders keeps cash flow steady.

Price all your change orders promptly and push for quick approval. Communicate costs and associated values clearly to clients. This will prevent unpleasant surprises and allow for timely payments.

Step 9: Over-Communicate with Customers

Keeping clients informed prevents misunderstandings.

Communicate often and early about project options and benefits. Keep customers updated on schedule impacts and involve them in decisions. Over-communication ensures everyone is on the same page.

Step 10: Learn How to Negotiate

Effective negotiation retains customers and results in mutual gain.

Train your teams in what negotiating is and how to do it in a way that retains customers. Teach them to identify options that result in win-win outcomes. This skill is crucial for handling change orders, schedule adjustments, cost negotiations, and more.

Step 11: Retain a Construction Attorney

This is your last resort. Legal battles are slow, expensive, and can damage reputations.

Avoid the legal route whenever possible. If legal action becomes necessary, having a construction attorney can help navigate the complexities. But remember, prevention is always better than cure.

Conclusion

Project management is a difficult job. All aspects are challenging in today's environment. A successful project is delivered on time, on budget, with quality and safety, **and it generates positive cash flow.**

Tools like the liquidity indicator provide understanding and application of sound cash management for project managers.

The three key concepts for successful project management are:

1. Building the project correctly
2. Managing the cost to earn a profit
3. Ensuring the cash flow is positive

When your project has a positive cash flow, it gets noticed. When all projects are cash flow positive, the company's cash flow is best-in-class.

Chapter Takeaways

Here are the main takeaways for our chapter on becoming an effective accountant.

- The Accountant archetype is essential to your project's success. By forecasting and managing your budget well, you're setting yourself and your entire team up for a win.
- Use **construction best practices** to save your company millions of dollars in the long run.

- Practice **change management** to turn change from a risk to a positive opportunity.
- **Forecast** well so you can effectively budget for every expense on the project.

Becoming an effective accountant will help you save your company money and set you and your team up for success. Use this chapter as a guide for managing your project's finances with excellence.

CHAPTER EIGHT

The Business Developer

"Business, after all, is nothing more than a bunch of human relationships."

~ Lee Iacocca

When I first started out as a project manager, I was laser-focused on the projects right in front of me. I thought my job was to deliver on time, on budget, and with the highest quality. And while that's all true, I was missing something crucial—thinking about the next project, the one that would follow this one.

It wasn't until I had a conversation with a mentor that things started to shift for me. We were wrapping up a big project, and I was feeling pretty good about how things had gone. But my mentor asked me a simple question: "What's next?"

That question hit me hard. I realized I had been so focused on finishing the project that I hadn't thought about the future. I hadn't thought about how this project could lead to the next one, how the relationships we were building now could open doors down the road. I hadn't seen the project as more than just a task to complete—but as an opportunity to build something bigger.

I remember a specific moment when this lesson really clicked. We were nearing the end of a project, and I made a point to sit down with the client. Instead of just talking about the project status, I asked them about their vision for the future. I listened to their challenges, their goals, and where they saw their business going.

In that conversation, I saw an opportunity to help them beyond the current project. I shared ideas on how we could solve their upcoming challenges, offered solutions, and positioned myself as someone who was invested in their long-term success—not just in getting this project done.

This experience taught me that every project is an opportunity—not just to deliver, but to develop. Each project is a chance to tell a story, solve a problem, and create an experience that naturally leads to the next one.

The transformation was complete when I saw how this approach changed my relationships with all my stakeholders. They started coming to me with their challenges before they even became projects, trusting that I could help them find the best path forward. I wasn't just a project manager anymore—I was a business developer, someone who was integral to their ongoing success.

This story matters because it shows that the current project is never just about the task at hand. It's an opportunity to build something bigger, to create a partnership that extends beyond the completion date. Every project is a stepping stone to the next, and how you finish today's work will determine the opportunities you create for tomorrow.

Why Does a Project Manager Need to be a Business Developer?

Future projects are just as important as the current one.

In construction, every project is an opportunity—to innovate, expand, and make a mark. While guaranteeing the project's success is vital, it's also crucial to think about what's next. While there may or may not be dedicated employees to the business development function, everyone who has a client-facing responsibility participates in business development.

As a project manager, nurturing client relationships and closing deals often falls to you and the leaders of your firm. Business development and marketing professionals assist, but those performing the work and managing projects are best positioned to build and maintain these relationships.

You play a pivotal role in driving business development. Every phone conversation, email, and meeting contributes to your firm's brand, drives future business opportunities, fulfills or discovers client expectations, and nurtures relationships.

Business Development is a key skill for influential project managers. It doesn't just happen before the project starts; it occurs throughout the entire project lifecycle. The most influential project managers develop business for the next project while working on the current one.

In this chapter, we'll discuss the characteristics of the Business Developer, and several tools to help you develop these skills: by examining the components of a relationship, learning 11 words that describe business development, being the guide, not the hero, and developing the skillset of effective storytelling.

Characteristics of The Business Developer

Think of the Business Developer like a farmer. Instead of just tending to the crops that are already growing, the farmer is always looking for new seeds to plant and more land to cultivate.

They are curious about what else they can grow and eager to find new markets where they can sell their produce. Similarly, a Business Developer in the AEC industry doesn't just focus on the task at hand. They're thinking of the next project.

The Business Developer, both authentic and likable, focuses on new opportunities, building lasting relationships, understanding client's needs, and thinking of ways to expand and improve the project's long-term outcome.

Let's take a look at how we can build positive relationships so you can develop the natural business opportunities around you.

How to Build Relationships

Relationships are key to your success and the success of any team.

When you recognize that relationships are paramount, you will prioritize building strong relationships with everyone around you.

A healthy workplace culture is one where people have positive relationships with each other. It's a place where people can trust each other, listen to each other, respect each other, and influence each other.

In contrast, a workplace where relationships are strained and toxic can be a recipe for disaster. Therefore, it's crucial to focus on building healthy relationships in the workplace.

Here, we'll dive into the ultimate relationship tool. It focuses on Trust, Listen, Respect, and Influence, to help you grow healthy workplace relationships.

What is a Relationship?

Think about someone you know. Do you have a good relationship with them? How do you measure whether or not you have a good relationship with them?

It's more than just greeting each other politely; it goes deeper than that.

To succeed in anything you are trying to do, you need to build strong relationships with those you depend on to accomplish your mission. Without relationships, we don't have a team.

Think about the people in your life that you really have a good relationship with. Maybe this is someone you work with. Or it could be someone in your community. Anyone in your life you really like.

When they ask you for help, what do you do? You help them. But what if you are busy? Really, really busy? When they ask for help, what do you do? You help them. That's the power of relationships. If we care about the other person enough, it doesn't matter how busy we are. We will find the time to help them.

Now consider the opposite. Think about the people in your life that you don't like. We all have them. When they ask you for something, what do you do? Most people won't do it. Usually, we won't help someone we dislike. Or we don't put much effort into helping them.

Obviously, that hurts them because they don't get the help from you that they need. But because they're a member of your team, that also hurts you! This is why you should strive to build strong relationships with everyone in your world—every person who impacts or could impact your mission.

How to Quantify a Relationship

How do you quantify your relationship with others rather than someone you simply "like" or "dislike"?

Ask yourself:

- Do you trust them? Do they trust you?
- Do you listen to them? Do they listen to you?
- Do they respect you? Do you respect them?

- Do you have the ability to influence them? Do they have the ability to influence you?

A relationship is built upon these four things:

1. Trust
2. Listen
3. Respect
4. Influence

If you don't have these things with someone, you don't have a relationship with them. In order to get these things from others, you have to give them first.

When you have a high level of trust with someone, when you listen to them, when you show them respect, when you allow them to influence you, they are far more likely to accept your feedback.

This is all the more powerful when they know that you care about them, that you are trying to help them and have their best interests in mind.

Tool #1 The 4 Components to a Relationship

Most leaders struggle to define relationships and don't understand how to build them.

Here's how you should think about and use this tool:

1. Maintain a Foundation of TRUST

Trust is the foundation of any relationship. Always tell the truth and deliver on your promises. Don't just *act* trustworthy, but actively trust your team as well. If you trust them to take ownership and make decisions, then they'll perform better. People rise to what you expect of them. If you expect your teammates to be trustworthy and responsible, they'll rise to that expectation. You also need to trust their input. Listen to them and don't get defensive when they push back.

2. LISTEN & Speak Last

Effective listening is non-negotiable in building relationships. Talk less, and listen more. When someone talks to you, show them that you're genuinely listening to what they have to say. When you do speak, make sure it's with intelligence. Check out my chapter on being an effective communicator to improve your speaking skills so others listen to you.

3. RESPECT Your Team & Earn Their Respect

Respect is mandatory for healthy work relationships. Lead by example and show respect to everyone, even those with different opinions. Be humble and respect your team's input. By creating a culture of mutual respect, you'll be able to build a positive and stable environment.

4. INFLUENCE & Be Influenced

Use your influence wisely and only when necessary. Don't just see it as your job to influence others. *Be* influenced by the brilliance of others on your team. Allowing others to influence you shows that you respect and value your teams' opinions. This leads to more productive and positive relationships.

This relationship tool (Trust, Listen, Respect, and Influence) helps leaders build healthy workplace relationships. You do this by trusting others, listening to them, showing them respect, allowing yourself to be influenced by them, and demonstrating that you care about them.

Remember, when you give and build healthy relationships, you give your team the best chance to succeed and continue working with your customers.

Let's take a moment to look at 11 words that accurately describe business development.

Tool #2 Business Development in 11 Words

I gathered myself and created a simple list of words that align with the chronological process of what I (and all you other business development leaders out there) do on a daily basis. These words are:

1. *Identify*
2. *Engage*
3. *Listen*
4. *Understand*
5. *Respond*
6. *Inform*
7. *Pursue*
8. *Affirm*
9. *Win*
10. *Fortify*
11. *Cultivate*

That's it... the 11 words that best describe the entire business development process.

Now, let's take them one at a time to clarify what they mean.

1. IDENTIFY

The first thing we all need to do is identify a prospective client and determine if they're a good fit for your firm (and if they'll eventually have interesting projects). No matter the client or owner organization, somebody must stand up and say "Hey, why aren't we working with them?"

Hopefully, you're part of the strategic planning process and there are champions created to establish optimum market share with each top client or preferred service market.

2. ENGAGE

Engage with prospective clients through trusted partners, events, or a phone call. Aim for a face-to-face meeting with a decision-maker or influencer.

Avoid sounding salesy; focus on building a meaningful.

3. LISTEN

Once you're engaged and in front of your prospective client, you clearly want to organize the conversation around your phone call or whatever inspired them to set the meeting. It may sound cliché, but listening is your most important activity.

Make the client comfortable so they talk and share valuable information. Everything they share can and should be used in the future to develop the relationship.

4. UNDERSTAND

Just as important as being listened to, clients want and need to be understood.

From the first meeting and beyond, you need to make sure you fully understand their goals, interests, ideas, likes, and dislikes.

Use phrases like, "So what you're saying is…" or "That's interesting, tell me more about…" to clarify and build trust.

The better you understand them, the better you can do what comes next.

5. RESPOND

Whether it's during your initial meetings or as part of a follow-up regimen, you must now start the effort of doing what you say you're going to do.

For any information, introductions, or activities that you've offered, you must follow through exactly as you promised… if not better or faster than anticipated.

Responsiveness is crucial during both the courting stage and ongoing projects. It never goes away.

6. INFORM

The best business developers aspire to excel at informing. You want to have the reputation with your clients that you're always looking for opportunities to enlighten them with industry trends, interesting events, or recent lessons learned.

You want to become their **trusted advisor.** That's the ultimate position you want to gain with your clients and, again, it takes constant effort to prove your value and worth to them and their needs.

7. PURSUE

This step happens when the right project comes along with your prospective clients and you decide to go for it.

Hopefully, you've already completed your go/no-go process. Now it's time to pursue the right projects with your prospective clients.

Business development, marketing, and the design or project management team must be fully inspired to win this project by:

1. Understanding all the client's issues
2. Caring about the impact of the project to its users
3. Knowing qualifications only got you here, they won't win the project.

Inspire clients to want to work with you, not just your resume.

8. AFFIRM

From the first paragraph of your proposal's cover letter to the closing statement of your presentation, sprinkle as much of the intelligence you've gained from the client since your first meeting.

Now you can prove you've listened by acknowledging what you've learned they care about the most; affirming how you will help make their vision happen; then affirming why your people, culture, and process match so well with theirs.

9. WIN

This is the goal you've been looking for ever since you decided (a long time ago) that you wanted to work with a new client. If you've followed the previous steps conscientiously, you'll likely get the results you're striving for.

Effective business development leads to wins, not just sales. Focus on the client, project purpose, and users, not just your firm.

10. FORTIFY

Now you have a new client. The business development process is not over, not by a long shot.

Focus on earning client loyalty through regular feedback and performance reviews. Find a good spot during each project to find out how your team is performing in the eyes of the client. Don't wait until after the project is complete, as that could be too late to fix a possible fractured relationship that was never shared.

Quick tip: **It's not what you do. It's how and why you do it.**

Focus your differentiating messages around your people and culture, as well as the lessons learned that only come from your specific experiences.

11. CULTIVATE

Engage, listen, understand, respond, and inform continuously. Don't wait until the end of a project to ask for more work. If not, you might have to start from scratch with that client.

As you execute your projects, make sure you do everything you can to maintain your preferred status because believe me, many other firms are trying to take that position away from you.

Between and during every step we've discussed, there's one key phrase or sentiment that must be shared consistently, and that's "Thank you!"

Never stop saying it and never stop sharing your appreciation. Celebrate new project awards and view them as wins, not sales.

By embracing the Business Developer archetype, you make sure that the projects you manage today lead to more opportunities tomorrow. This next tool is essential to developing your ability to connect with clients.

Tool #3 Storytelling

Every project brings an opportunity to tell an incredible story. An observation from having the privilege of spending time with some incredible leaders:

Storytelling is EVERYTHING.

World-changing CEOs aren't the smartest people in their organizations. They are exceptional at aggregating data and communicating it simply & effectively. **Data in, story out.**

Believe it or not, as a project manager you are a storyteller. You are responsible for administering the project and narrating the story along the way. **If you can build that storytelling skill, you'll always be valuable.**

Every marketer or business developer will tell you, if a customer does not remember your message and repeat it, it is likely not very effective marketing. People will remember and repeat good stories.

The best project managers are aware of the story, the characters involved and use their story to lead into the next opportunity.

Every good story has (7) key elements:

1. The Character: There is always a main character, who is the hero. Make sure your work stories place your client in the role of the main character and hero.
2. The Problem: The hero runs into a challenge or obstacle. This is the problem of your story.
3. The Guide: The hero meets a guide who provides wisdom and assistance to overcome problem. You, the construction professional, are the guide.
4. The Plan: The guide offers a plan that will help the hero overcome their problem.

5. The Challenge: Once a plan is laid out for the hero, the guide must call the hero to action. This call to action is the hero's challenge.
6. The Failure Avoidance: Once the hero engages the challenge, the guide helps them avoid failure.
7. The Success: The hero overcomes the problem and experiences success. The hero's life is changed for the better.

The more the industry leans into video, client experience, thought leadership, and content marketing, the more valuable good storytelling will be.

What stories do you have to tell? What's the story of your current project?

When telling the story of your current project, there's one important thing you need to remember.

Tool #4 Be The Guide, Not The Hero

The most common error many project managers and business developers make when telling their story is placing themselves in the role of the hero.

I cannot emphasize this enough: the client is the hero of the story!

When you make yourself or your firm the hero, the client loses interest in your story. Besides, when most other competing firms and project managers are making themselves the heroes, you simply sound like everyone else. Nothing differentiates you or makes your story memorable.

You are the **guide** who assists the hero.

You are the Yoda and the client is Luke Skywalker.

When creating and telling the story of your project, the challenges and obstacles you've overcome, the problems you've solved, turn the story toward the client and talk about the challenges *they* overcame and the problems you helped *them* solve.

This may take some extra courage to present to your leadership. For decades, the stories of AEC firms have been ego-centric, placing our brilliant design professionals as the heroes of their own stories. This must flip!

Besides, who doesn't want to be Yoda?

Make sure you have framed the client as the hero and your project team as the guide.

What you will notice is that framing yourself as the guide assisting the hero is actually a stronger position to manage, lead, and communicate from. It's a classic win/win/win scenario, making you an even more influential manager.

Chapter Takeaways

Here are the main takeaways for our chapter on becoming an effective business developer.

- By becoming a great **Business Developer,** you ensure that you continue to land clients and stay in business.
- By knowing and navigating the **components of a relationship,** you'll be able to develop positive connections with the folks you work with.
- By remembering the **11 words of business development,** you'll be able to form relationships with any potential client who comes your way.

- When discussing a project with a client, make sure that you present yourself **as the guide, not the hero.** The client is always the hero, and they'll see you in a more positive light when you acknowledge that in the stories you tell.
- **By telling this project's story effectively,** you and your excellent work will be remembered in your client's mind.

Becoming a business developer will help you build positive relationships with your clients and land more jobs. Use this chapter as a guide to help you develop the relational tools you need for positive interactions with your clients.

CONCLUSION

Project management is one of the hardest industries to conquer. But you didn't get into this industry to fold under the stress—you got where you are today by bucking up, being tough, and tackling obstacles as they arise. This book is really just a guide to help you address the obstacles of the job.

By taking the skills you've learned in this book, you'll be able to develop into the communicator, enforcer, builder, leader, attorney, accountant, and business developer that you need to be in order to succeed.

- **As a communicator** you'll be able to take what's in your mind and showcase it well enough that your team has the exact same information in their minds as well. You can grow in this archetype by identifying your key message, preparing for your meetings, using visual aids, and growing as an active listener.
- **As an enforcer** you'll be able to hold your team accountable so they achieve the highest amount of excellence. You can grow in this archetype by setting clear expectations, confronting poor behavior early, and creating scoreboards and accountability logs.
- **As a builder,** you'll be able to problem solve obstacles on the job and hold your team accountable to the highest degree of excellence in the industry. You can develop this archetype by growing in constructability, avoiding waste, and understanding MEP systems.
- **As a leader,** you'll be able to inspire your team to do their absolute best. You can develop this archetype by changing your perspective so your vision for the project is at the

forefront always, creating an environment of ownership with your team, and being the captain that your team needs.

- **As an attorney,** you'll be able to advocate for yourself, your team, and your clients by knowing the contents of the contracts you sign. You can grow in this archetype by remembering that your biggest enemy is your own biases and creating a risk register.
- **As an accountant,** you'll be able to forecast and stick to a realistic budget with each project you take on. You can develop this archetype by learning to forecast well, creating a cost report, and accelerating your project's finances.
- **As a business developer,** you'll be able to create positive relationships with clients, turning your one project into several. You can develop this archetype by learning the components of a relationship, being the guide, not the hero, and learning how to tell your story as a project manager.

Remember the assessment wheel we looked at in chapter one? Take a moment and revisit that picture. Analyze your own assessment wheel and remember that uneven areas show where you need more focus. This month, pick two areas that you would like to improve in. Define what a 9 or 10 looks like for each section that you want to work on. Then, set realistic, time-bound goals to achieve that perfect ten. If you lead a team, you can involve them and revisit the exercise 1-2 times a year to track your progress. Remember, round wheels roll best!

Self-improvement is a continuous climb, and with each step, there's more to learn and adapt.

By using these seven archetypes, you'll be able to enter the top 1% of project managers. Take the tools in this book, apply them to your career, and watch as your projects, outcomes, and community start to transform.

It's time to quit being a project manager and become a project leader.

Want to read more about becoming an influential project leader? Scan the QR code below to sign up for my free weekly newsletter! Every Tuesday, get one strategic idea, framework, tip, or tool delivered straight to your inbox to help you lead successful projects with confidence.

BIBLIOGRAPHY

40+ Project Management Statistics. (2023, August 16). Exploding Topics. https://explodingtopics.com/blog/project-management-stats

Wells, R. (2023, November 10). *25 Million Project Managers In Demand As Median Salaries Soar To $120,000*. Forbes. https://www.forbes.com/sites/rachelwells/2023/11/10/25-million-project-managers-in-demand-as-median-salaries-soar-to-120k/

www.ingramcontent.com/pod-product-compliance
Lightning Source LLC
Chambersburg PA
CBHW071052240526
45471CB00015B/1642